thoughts from a GRUMPY innovator

written & illustrated by costas papaikonomou

This is the second edition, June 2013

Twitter: @grumpyinnovator
Email: costas@grumpyinnovator.com
Web: grumpyinnovator.com

ISBN 978-90-818800-0-8

to Patricia, Spiro and Dimi

who melt my grumpiness away, instantly.

[If the grass weren't greener on the other side, humanity would still be in caves with no intention to mow any of it.]

Kudos

“9/10 ... it also turns out his book is touched with genius ... aphorisms, many of which are as pointed as they are funny. If only all business books could be this entertaining.”
Tim Hulse
Editor @ British Airways, Business Book of the Month

★★★★ - ”This book is a *lot* of fun.”
BookIdeas.com

“Flippantly Flipping Fabulous. An antidote of sunshine for true innovators and intrapreneurs struggling in the web of corporate ambiguity!”
Arun Prabhu,
Commercial Innovation Director @ Arla Foods

★★★★ - “A collection of thoughts and observations regarding the bizarre and illogical world of commercial innovation”
San Francisco Book Review

"I was grumpy wishing I had written it. It now sits officially on the top of the 'books I will steal from shamelessly' pile.”
Dave McCaughan,
Director of Strategic Planning @ McCann

”This book is packed with witty observations that make serious points"
Frank Dillon
Business Editor @ The Irish Times

“...the kind of read where you will find yourself laughing at the wit, or agreeing sadly...”
John P. Muldoon’s Innovation Blog

”Funny, witty, insightful and fresh but most importantly... 200% spot on !"
Diamantis Economou
Global Group Marketing Director @ DeLonghi Group

“Fun, easy read on avoiding & navigating the challenges companies face today in evolving their businesses. Written with an entrepreneurial feel most true innovators can relate to!! :-)”
Rick Castanho, UX Strategist @ Lowes

“Highly entertaining and raises some disturbing points on innovation and corporations within a lively context of professional self-parody and humour.”
Gavin Dickinson
Consumer & trade insights @ GDCTI

“Innovation and humour go together excellently, as Costas Papaikonomou convincingly proves.”
Technology Weekly

“Ah, the sweet smell of nails hit squarely on the head.”
Darrell Mann
Systematic Innovation E-zine

★★★★ - ”Innovative and Not Very Grumpy. Behind the wit, and what makes the humor shine through the brief remarks, is his earnestness about and depth of knowledge of his subject.”
Portland Book Review

Thoughts from a Grumpy Innovator

This little book is the narcissistic result of posting thoughts onto Twitter™ over a number of years, mostly on the topic of mass market innovation.

A couple of themes have emerged, which form the chapters of this book – each with a central narrative, thought or plain grump.

My interest is in the intrinsic, systemic reasons commercial innovation works the way it does. Which I can summarize for you right here as being quite *odd*, to say the least.

If you're looking for a business management book with clear-cut tips and tricks, then I'm sorry. You won't find an extensive list of innovation success stories to copy, nor an Innovate-O-Matic toolbox to plunder. There is no 12-step process that will guarantee a successful launch of your new idea.

So I'm afraid I can't promise you'll make millions after reading this book, but I do hope you'll smile every now and then.

Premise: I'm grumpy and I shouldn't be

Anyone celebrating the tenacity of successful innovators is probably ignoring the far larger number of tenacious idiots pursuing bad ideas. If you think about the classic description of what character traits help people succeed in turning an innovative idea into a profitable business stream – winners and losers at this particular game are frighteningly similar:

- ***Dogged determination***
- ***Blind devotion to their idea***
- ***Unshakable confidence, against all odds***

There must be a fine line between getting it very right or very wrong. In fact, I think there's a paradox hidden in there.

Companies are structured entities, with defined procedures and efficient processes that ensure things get done. Even the messiest of businesses are organized to some level. In stark contrast, the *reality* they operate in is unpredictable, fluid, ugly and most of all: immense. In this simple contrast lies a beautiful paradox: it is the reason there will always be new opportunities & needs for new things *and* it is the main reason for failing at successfully doing so. The attributes that guarantee new opportunities are the opposite of what an efficient corporate system thrives upon.

The chart on the next page shows how the four capabilities crucial to running a business are hampered in the context of innovation[1]. Within the neatly controlled corporate ecosystem, they do as they're asked to and all is fine – as long as they keep looking inward.

---

[1] *Yes, you can slice business up many other ways too. But this particular way happens to work well for my profession.*

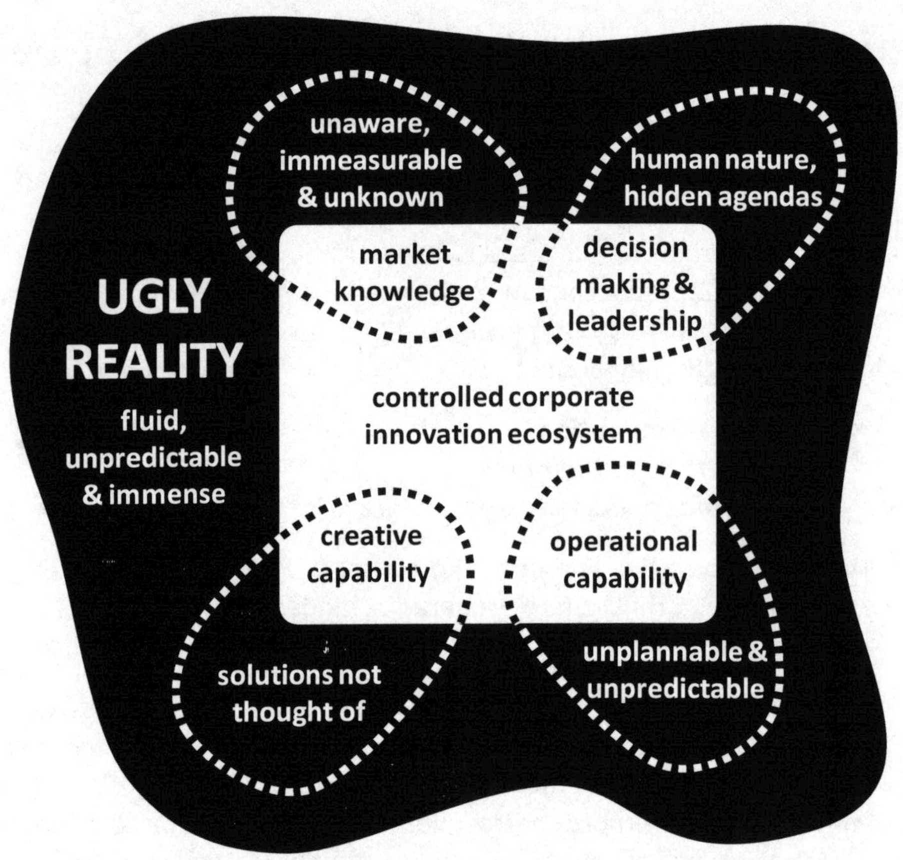

I've found most of the failures in innovation can be brought back to individuals and teams in denial of the reality outside of their campus walls, totally unnecessarily.

This little book holds some of the thoughts I had seeing this happen. If you have experience in the innovation arena, you may recognize attitudes, situations and odd behaviours. Don't worry, we'll keep those our little secret.

Costas Papaikonomou
The Hague, June 2013

The Art Of Beanbags & Funny Hats

I KNOW IT'S JUST A BOX. BUT WAIT 'TILL YOU HEAR THE SINGLE-MINDED BENEFIT.

The Art Of Beanbags & Funny Hats

Every solution has a problematic history, by definition. In that sense, the skills behind successful innovation could be framed as the ability to create solutions for problems before anyone realizes what a nuisance they are. Successful innovation is not about dreaming up what would be science fiction today, but about foreseeing what will be plain vanilla tomorrow.

You can imagine most creative professionals do not find that thought particularly motivating, which is why such a large chunk of this discipline appears to be about putting the 'art' of being creative up on an ever higher pedestal than the output it generates. Much of the world of innovation is populated by creative gurus, visionary high priests who scatter riddles across 2x2 diagrams to paint your future portfolio. Well, implement creativity like a religion and you'll need miracles to be successful.

Breakthrough ideas often feed creative egos, not consumer needs. If anything, successful new products and services are like the weather; about 90% the same as yesterday's products. This isn't to say the world needs no game changing innovation; it's merely that too many businesses waste time looking *outside* the box when their market still has plenty room left to grow and differentiate *inside* it.

For some of the world's leading companies and brand teams, success seems based on historical serendipities, luck, or lack of competition. Nevertheless stupendous amounts of money are wasted on turning an innovation project into a show.

Maybe creative capability is genuinely seen as something much more difficult than it really is? Then again, if Edison really meant it being 1% inspiration and 99% perspiration he would have invented deodorant. Or GoreTex. What's making this all so difficult?

- ***A belief you need to be uncomfortable to work outside your comfort zone**. Funny hats, beanbags and humiliating 'energizers'. A whole industry has grown around the mantra that in order for people to take creative risk, they should be made to feel even more uneasy than they already are.*

- ***Features rather than benefits?** The first decade of the new millennium brought high-end software and technology into consumers' daily lives, in a way previously unheard of. With it came an insatiable drive for new features in order to provide marginal difference between devices and social media, a trend which seems to be trickling down into physical mass markets. What happened to thinking about benefits first? If anything, added features often introduce another hurdle between a consumer and the benefit they're trying to get from a product. They also distract attention from the core that's attracting consumers to your products.*

- ***Re-inventing predecessors' wheels.** In many corporate ecosystems the responsibility for innovation lies with the marketing department, a discipline known for high job rotation. Which from an innovation standpoint is fine, as long as the track record is kept diligently. And often it isn't. New marketing & brand managers waste plenty of their time redeveloping ideas that have bombed many times before.*

- ***Believing your own spin.** In mature FMCG categories, the reality is that everyone needs to push the envelope on what can be claimed in order to stand out from the crowd. But the line between substantiated claims and spin is thin. No problem. Think homeopathy. In practice this leads to claims that* sound credible *in respect of the brand equity or previous claims, rather than being based on new developments. And that's when a credible myth all too easily becomes the new benchmark for truth.*

- ***Marketing executive's lives and their consumers' lives couldn't be further apart.*** *Having empathy with your target consumer does not mean bringing to market only the products you'd buy yourself. On the contrary. Corporate professionals dealing with mass market innovation tend to belong to a society's top 2% income level, with the other 98% being their target. This target is seldom as interested in 'on-the-go' or 'stress relief' or 'personalization' as one may hope.*

So what to do? Well, first of all assume there is a solution for any creative problem and trust that it won't require black magic to uncover it.

- ***Make time, not space.*** *You don't need to be in a Hungarian lakeside castle to be creative. In fact, the environment is mostly irrelevant as long as it's comfortable – that's why beds and bathtubs ignite new ideas. What you need most is* TIME. *Uninterrupted time to work on the innovation task, alone or as a group – to understand the problem, the context and to work on solutions. If you do your homework, a couple of days is often enough to crack even the toughest nuts.*

- ***An un-filtered look at the (consumer) context****. All you need is some rigor in pinpointing what the real needs are, for relevant answers to pop out painlessly. Real insight carries far. Note this involves more listening and reading to what consumers actually say and less reading of macro-economic trends or your brand vision deck.*

- ***Cherish the small incremental ideas.*** *Most growth challenges do not require breakthrough solutions. Give small ideas a chance.*

- ***Reality first – then brand equity.*** *Stay in touch with the physical attributes of your product before getting carried away by what you wish were possible. The touch, the smell, the chemistry, the taste, the sounds... Nothing beats a trip to your factory and R&D lab before getting to work on a consumer problem.*

Maybe all this is best summarized as follows:

Keep these …

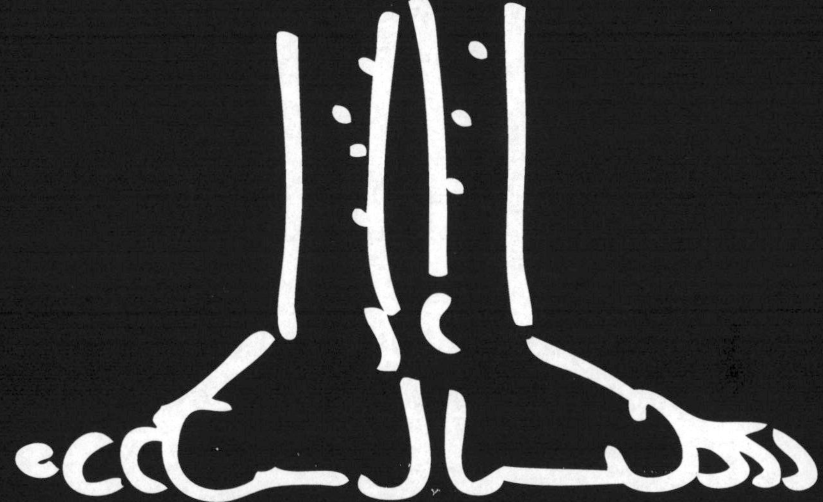

… on the ground.

Wishful thinking and blue-sky ideation are absolutely fine, but they are a transfer station, not the end destination of your effort. Even the wildest ideas must come back to earth in order to become part of an operational process that can make a business thrive.

"I just found out someone else had exactly the same idea before me" - poor sod uncovering the truth about all ideas.

Great innovations versus duds... One is full of flaws, a budget vampire, ruins careers, virtually no chance of success. The other is a dud.

Our best flashes of inspiration happen when having shower, which is really practical with the 99% perspiration then kicking in.

[Solutions without problems are even worse time vampires than problems without solutions.]

Just like you shouldn't shop for food on an empty stomach, you shouldn't innovate on an empty development funnel. Anything would then be good enough.

"The heart of a lion and the mind of a dandelion" – great recipe for creative success.

Good ideas and bad ideas have one thing in common: at first glance, both often look like bad ideas. Or was it the other way around?

Ask not how to make the future more futuristic, ask instead how to make the past more old-fashioned.

Planning to have an idea while sitting at your desk is no different from answering emails while having a shower.

If you're wondering whether that idea is good enough, it probably isn't. If only because your insecurity would stand in the way of bringing even the best idea to market.

Industries succeeding through in-the-box thinking: pizza delivery, caskets, multiple choice input devices and flight data recording.

An un-creative person in a beanbag with a funny hat & a Hawaiian shirt on is still un-creative. But now armed with false confidence.

Don't reinvent a wheel that merely needs reframing.

Step 1 to finding a solution is realising there is one. Step 0 is admitting you haven't got one.

If you find yourself needing the word "because" more than once when introducing a new idea to an audience, either the idea or the audience need sharpening.

The good thing that success and failure have in common is that they both break the status quo.

Your Blue Sky innovation may have patches of rain.

There are no bad ideas, only unappreciative audiences.

Like with children, you sometimes need to discipline your ideas to ensure they grow into mature beings.

Enlightenment comes from small, sweet observations, yoga, Buddha and lamp posts.

Good ideas tend to take more time to develop than bad ones. Sadly, spending forever developing an idea doesn't guarantee it'll be good.

Only in innovation can evolution and creationism comfortably coexist.

Slapping 'New Formula' or 'Improved Recipe' onto an existing product's label is the innovator's equivalent of writer's block.

When encountering a road block on an innovation roadmap, finding the solution will also transform the path itself and lead to a new destination.

There are those who see their bodies as convenient carriers to move their brain around; and those who just see their bodies.

There is a fine line beyond which asking lots of questions shifts from being a token of curiosity to one of paralyzing insecurity.

The story of this particular innovation project I'm in would make a fantastic musical.

Like real children, ideas need most attention when they're tired and start annoying everyone.

WE CREATED THIS COLLAGE TO EXPRESS CONSUMERS' EMOTIONAL EXPERIENCE OF "1KG"

If your new ideas aren't impressing the old folks, share some of your old ideas with the new folks.

Don't expect a serendipitous solution when, you're concentrating really hard to find one.

Jobs where creativity is frowned upon: airline pilot, doctors, taxi driver, accountant, judge, taxman, garbage collector, son-in-law.

[If at first you succeed, try, try again anyway.]

The bottom line is that 'systematized creativity' is like 'creative accounting': it's a bit naughty and everyone secretly wants some.

Prehistoric Man learned how to catch fish. Industrial Age Man learned how to catch and sell lotsa fish. Z-Gen Man learned to tweet #Where2BuyShushi.

Big ideas have only small audiences, initially.

Great ideas usually come in pairs. First a fabulous one, then an even more fabulous one. But only if you don't lose your cool after the first one.

When you bump into a massive barrier... you have in fact found what will eventually become the way forward.

On left/right brain modes. When chatting on the phone... Should I hold my wife to my left ear and my accountant to my right?

Mediocre idea? Write it on the back of a napkin, photograph it and project it full-screen in PowerPoint. If it still fails, it IS mediocre.

Amazing how Einstein didn't need Einstein quotes for inspiration.

Beware of breakthrough concepts that are designed to feed their creators' egos instead of consumer needs. They can be deceitfully appealing.

People want holes, not drills. Sorry, I mean hooks, not holes. No, decorations on walls, not hooks. No, a nice house!

A compromise is not a solution; it's not even supposed to be. Unless you manage to turn it into a feature and call it a 'hybrid'.

Evolution: the path from A to B. Revolution: the leap from A to C. Game Changer: the path from A to sliced bread.

Things that are exceptionally fast tend to also be exceptionally fragile. And exceptionally far off mark when aimed incorrectly.

"Temporarily removes nagging sense of guilt" would work as an on-pack claim on most food products. Does anyone know if EFSA will allow this?

* SPOILER ALERT * Box-o-chocolate style concepts to personalize product experience will BOMB in concept tests, except in Chocolates category.

It's amazing how much stuff you sometimes need to remove from a three word idea headline, in order to get through to the ten word essence.

The level of brilliance of an idea is not defined by the idea itself, but by the audience exposed to it. So choose your audience wisely. I mean dumbly.

When wondering what benefits to add to your proposition, don't forget to remove a few too.

The perfect packaging is one that's made itself obsolete. Yet the ambition to develop 'nothing' is a leap too far for most pack developers.

All the lateral, right brain thinking I've been doing has made my left brain feel constrained & stifled. Time for out-of-the-box reasoning.

On the development timeline, innovation is the bit that happens in between celebrations.

As a lone brand manager, you sometimes find yourself lost, lacking ideas, vision. And THAT's when the bean bag & post-its business gets you.

I wonder if the length of an innovation pipeline correlates with the attention span of the people responsible for filling it?

If you're allowed to bring just one thing to creative problem solving workshop; bring an answer.

OK, time for some of my own medicine. From now on, I pledge to have 10% better ideas.

Great, so we selected the sensible, safe idea from that batch of wacky concepts. Now let's build some fun into it, because it's a bit bland. #NeverGonnaHappen

Fact: workshop warm-up with armpit farts and alphabet burping does not raise a group's collaborative creativity, but man is it funny.

Well, as a last resort when looking for new USP's, you could choose to use your own product for a while & find out first hand.

Does your new idea look equally attractive with helmet hair and without make-up? Then don't hold back and embrace the future.

[**Test your true love of an idea by considering having it tattooed.**]

Make sure to have plenty of sex before an ideation workshop because even if you then have no ideas, you'll still have had plenty of sex.

Bad ideas can be cunningly disguised as good ones. Be prepared and arm yourself with the infallible power of hindsight.

LSD is pretty bad at creativity, unless you give a human as a tool.

[**Try explaining the value of a single-minded concept benefit to schizophrenic marketing manager.**]

Relying on your 1st idea as your best idea is like expecting the idea of the century to come in the 1st decade.

No two snowflakes are alike. Ditto for cornflakes and skin flakes or any other flake you may meet today.

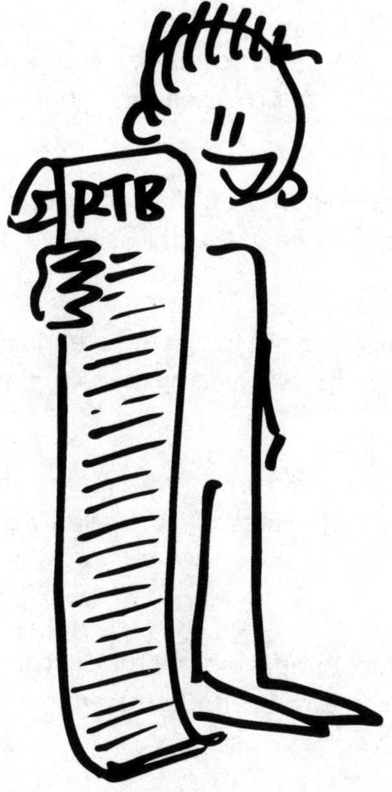

Funny hats and beanbags in innovation sessions will help you creatively mess up your hair and wrinkle your trousers.

If you look hard and concentrate enough, you'll miss the solutions right under your nose.

If your product name sounds like something from a 50's monster movie, a 60's SF movie, or a 70's exploitation movie... Reconsider.

Don't clutter a great idea with too much "Reason To Believe". You'll look like you're trying to cover up something, like the crooks in those old Columbo episodes.

Use it or lose it: a truth for your creative mind, your best people, your muscle mass, your front row seat and your car keys.

The success of an idea depends on the audience, the timing and the capability to manage cash flow. Much less the idea itself.

Creative Problem Solving is the intriguing arena where complex technical problems can be resolved by blistering air guitar solos.

The fact you have nothing better doesn't mean what you have is good enough. Which is of course what originally drove us to walking upright.

Probably the single most important factor in progressing difficult innovation initiatives is getting enough sleep, for all involved.

When was the last time you surprised someone with a present they asked for? Co-creation works by uncovering needs, not by asking for ideas.

85% of inventors are too optimistic about the chances of success for their big idea. 10% are realistic. The successful 5% are very lucky.

Knowledge and innovation are fuelled by curiosity, so their greatest inhibitor is not ignorance but apathy. Or worse, bigotry. "

MOM, DAD – HE'S A CREATIVE.

It was a dark and stormy night..." - Marketing manager about to write a massively verbose consumer insight statement.

"Well, 2x2's are so old hat of course. Experience the raw power of our new 3x3" - boardroom consultant up-selling.

Newton explained that a system in balance won't accelerate nor decelerate. Go figure, work-life balance coaches.

If you can't explain your proposition with only hand gestures and maybe a crayon, make it simpler. Practice in a foreign language.

Inside every grey office mouse sits a vibrant creative soul, screaming to please be left inside where it's nice and quiet.

Hinged cell phones went extinct because of the discomfort for men with sideburns.

I'm writing this Organic Fair Trade food concept and need your help. Is "moral superiority" an emotional or rational consumer benefit?

In concept development, one word often says more than a thousand pictures.

I suspect most people complaining about lack of good ideas simply don't know what a good idea looks like.

Innovation success is as much defined by bravery as it is by the quality of the idea. Having opposable thumbs helps too.

Of course, for dreams to be broken, they require some structural integrity first.

No, you can't go out and look for something random. It wouldn't be random, would it?

"Let's revitalize this category with a new product everyone will love" – team embarking on product development which everyone will hate.

Yo Momma innovate so bad she lined up at the dole office to collect her concept's benefits.

Perfectionists and slackers have in common that neither knows when something is good enough.

Whoever talks about creative thought being as liberating as flying is deliberately excluding the analogy of endless runway taxiing.

Be aware that the big idea that will make you millions may currently be disguised as the rattling prototype that doesn't really work. Yet.

Get your final copy written by a native speaker; but not before the underlying proposition is done by a foreigner with half the vocabulary.

"Now watch me chart your future portfolio by using this amazing 2x2 matrix" - opening sentence to pseudo-scientific marketing extravaganza.

Innovation success factors: total dedication, long hours, your last money – they'll guarantee it wasn't lack of effort that thwarted your Big Idea.

Ideagnosia - the inability to recognize a good idea right in front of you.

You can't cancel out bad ideas by adding good ones. That just doubles your workload.

Speeding up an ideation workshop fearing creativity will run out is like speeding up painting a room fearing the paint will run out.

Set your objective clearly, focus, be confident, work hard and you'll be sure to miss the better opportunities that pop up on the way there.

Water and Air have remarkably low PR value as magic ingredients; even though they're two of the very few we actually can't do without.

[The quality of an idea is defined by the sender, the receiver and the amount of noise on the line.]

Imagine someone has to use your user-friendly feature 20 times an hour, 8 hours a day. Is it then still user-friendly or just fancy looking?

Stretching far out of the box and then raking it back in works great for innovative ideas; but very poorly for romantic relationships.

Contrary to Archimedes' findings - when you're up shit creek, hot air sinks and dense, grounded stuff flies.

Things that struggle to find new owners in the 2nd hand market: toothbrushes, 35mm cameras, underwear and creative ideas. #NotInventedHere

I've just upgraded my lucky socks to lucky pyjamas. Hope my clients don't notice.

Creative Entropy - Once you've made something simple into a complicated mess, you can never make it simple again.

No matter what your creative facilitator wants you to do, you cannot focus outside the box. #HairSplitting

Creative revenge is best served bold.

Creating ideas alone is like drinking alone. Less fun, less productive, potentially embarrassing and a sign that something else is wrong.

Bottled iceberg & glacier water? I thought we were trying to keep those frozen. Or is it sustainable by freezing some Rhine tap water back?

SCREW THE INNOVATION FUNNEL.
I WANT TO GO HOME.

It's so easy to make it all very complicated.

If your big fab idea is so radically new there's nothing to compare it to, you have a massive positioning problem coming up.

From a constructive point of view, the row of windows in an airplane is like a massive perforated tear-strip to separate top & bottom halves.

Champagne for the winning idea. Real pain for what usually happens next.

Raising the innovative capability of a nation: Ask not what your country can do for you. Ask what you can do contrary.

The innovation space for new magic ingredients in food is about the size of the logic gap that both oxygen AND anti-oxidants are perceived as beneficial.

Only when facing deadlines do you finally notice the beauty of staring out the window watching the weather pass by.

[**Having to invent a new word to describe your idea is sometimes good, but usually very bad.**]

The ability to take ownership of something you didn't ask for is a mind-set to admire.

If you want the CMO to be happy, make sure the CFO is happy first.

Before launch, do check your original insight was a real one and not some spin you made up long ago just to get the project signed off.

Even in the most powerful and diverse ideation sessions, temptation calls to simply pick the new ideas that landed inside the box.

On word-smithing concepts. Ask yourself "will this really affect the final execution in any way?". Then find something useful to do.

[Hey positioning guru - what have you redone for me lately?!]

Funny how before social media, companies actually had to go out and speak with their consumers.

"Ceci n'est pas une pipe-ligne d'innovation!" - Magritte being really annoying in his first job in consumer goods.

The best R&D teams are happy to make the brand teams believe it's their own great idea. We can keep a secret.

The easiest place to start improving your products is reducing or removing the trade-offs of using it. Yes, there is always a trade-off.

"Would it generate enough excitement for a crowd funded business case?" - a good way to mentally check if your idea is truly breakthrough.

Aaargh. I always forget where I parked my ideas.

It takes three to Tango, unless one of the two can play the bandoneón while dancing.

[Big ideas go unnoticed, unless you sprinkle lots of small ideas around them as reference to highlight the difference.]

The question isn't if there's possibly a better idea (yes there will be), the question is if it'll be yours and if it's worth waiting for.

I have a hunch that successful artists are in fact successful businesspeople with an artsy hobby to fill the gaps between deals. #

Innovation oxymorons: "extensive brief", "exploratory focus group", "emergency procedure", "low-risk opportunity" and "creative process".

Hey breakthrough innovators - yes, you can bend the rules of law & regulation. You cannot bend the laws of physics.

Even with the best intent, brainstorming for problems is never helpful.

"He who looks up, sees no borders" - but does trip over the kids toys all the time.

I think I'll re-interpret Einstein's quote as "Take things as serious as possible, but not too serious".

Invite the whole team to evaluate your idea and I guarantee you'll hear reasons it won't work that you had never imagined possible.

If your design team's presentation is laid out in Comic Sans, tread carefully.

When working on breakthrough product innovation, don't forget to check if you have the brands to deliver them through.

"No - 'rewarding' and 'gratifying' are two VERY DIFFERENT emotional benefits!" - Never wordsmith concepts with a OCD marketer.

"We want something with an eye and a globe" - starting point for too many logo design briefs and end point for too many un-briefed designs.

[Are you re-writing that concept to convince your consumer or your market research department?]

Nice shirt! I see you fell for the "no iron" on-pack claim.

You know the R&D prototype presentation is going to be fun if the presenter puts in earplugs and steps back 6ft before pressing 'start'.

Beware of brand managers who talk eloquently and extensively about their brand, without referring to the actual products.

"This concept has enough substance to excite a homeopath"

Passion backed by numbers will always beat mere passion.

"It's SO annoying when people check emails during my presentation. Or worse, just start talking" - Stewardess after her flight safety instruction.

"Help, I'm A Celebrity Get Me Outta Here" - the attitude amongst most marketing managers working on the same brand for longer than 3 years.

Give me a reason why - and I'll give you a conflicting one.

A: "Let's do an innovation marathon!"
B: "That's our normal procedure."

"I'd like to do more strategic work; but I don't really have a plan on how to do this" - the irony is lost on the thousands of creatives saying this.

"6!! I NEED A 6th... NOW!!" - Desperate marketing manager whose quadruple promise has just been trumped by the competition's 5-in-1 claim.

"We need to explain our benefit with a broad, sweeping metaphor, consumers love that" - Marketer who needs to get more specific, quickly.

The modern equivalent of the classic concept format (insight-promise-RTB-tagline) is written as WTF-LOL-OMG-Like(x).

[You may need to go back through your notes a few times to find what you weren't looking for.]

I'm ditching the beanbags and funny hats. I hear it's much more effective to run creative workshops while driving, showering and sleeping.

The Evil Twin Of Operational Excellence

THE COST-OF-GOODS OF THIS PRODUCT IS ABSOLUTELY AWFUL. HOW ABOUT AERATING IT AND CALLING IT A MOUSSE?

The Evil Twin Of Operational Excellence

Operational Excellence - the mantra that came into fashion in the early nineties of the previous century and one that is still fanatically preached across the globe. This is the world of Lean, Six Sigma, 5s, TQM.

It assumes businesses thrive by being operationally perfect.

Paradoxically, many of the process superstars that grew to dominate their markets through Operational Excellence have fallen prey to its stillborn twin: *Systemic Inertia*. In a quest to raise profitability and short term reward, companies everywhere have been over-optimizing their business processes and ignoring an ancient planning truth: plan 80% with rigor and cunning, then leave 20% flexible for the Unpredictable. Scary stuff, because it requires reserving expensive resources that may end up not being used at all. Even worse, it may be abused in the most anti-operational horror known to process designers: improvisation.

Leadership teams grew blind to the fact the world around them is by nature unpredictable. They created a monster that leaves their business inflexible, unresponsive and in trouble. And the trouble accelerates, not just because of today's new economic reality, but for two systemic reasons as well.

- **Blinkered systems**. Masters of efficiency will be unaware they are in trouble until their relentlessly churning systems jam and it's way too late to correct course. Dell was the unrivalled master of assembling and delivering desktop computers to customized customer specification. But when the market interest abruptly shifted to laptops, Dell did not notice until stock started piling up in places it never had before. Had Dell been a little less 'perfect' on desktops and spent more resources on chasing (and failing) less profitable non-desktop market opportunities, it may have caught the laptop wave sooner. Similarly, the planet's most efficient manufacturing machine, Toyota, drove itself into unimaginable losses like a run-away train before it could tame the beast and adapt to the changed market dynamics.

- **Operator attitude**. The expertise required for Operational Excellence and the attitude required to successfully improvise are mutually exclusive. Businesses that accumulate pools of great process operators will naturally evolve into horrendous improvisers. And the more skewed resource pool, the more likely the one type will drive the other out of the organization as they tend to disagree on almost everything. So the better a business is equipped to accelerate profitability by Operational Excellence, the worse it will be at innovating and keeping an eye open for the next big opportunity. Just imagine what meetings are like in a room full of process operators once the systems have jammed. An operational mind-set tends to look for even further rigor in planning and stricter process controls, rather than questioning the output and the process itself.

Is there then no hope for Operational Excellence? Of course there is, and you can even dress up the solutions as old-school Operational Excellence so none of the accountants will notice. Here's what you do:

- **Fail faster**. Accelerating failure and dealing with regular small losses saves you from the life-threatening systemic bleeders. Do many small launches rather than few big ones. Ensure your production lines derail, jam or raise flags much faster when demand changes (even when it goes up). Operational Excellence systematically pushes business life into sameness, whilst it's the ability to notice, react to and create differences that help tap new opportunities.

- **Entrepreneurial attitude and incentives**. In the micro-cosmos of Operational Excellence, the processes become more important than the output, which is reflected in employees' KPI's across all levels and disciplines. Marketing Managers are rewarded for concepts' performance in market research rather than on shelf. Manufacturing Managers receive applause for improving asset efficiency, but not for smart use of the resulting idle time when they optimize capacity beyond market demand. Customer Service teams are increasingly good at providing their customers help in ways prescribed in the helpdesk operation manuals, but hopeless when confronted with a non-scripted problem.

Perhaps I can summarize this as

Not a machine ...

... but a dynamic system.

Increasing flexibility, being less operationally excellent will appear like a short term dip in process efficiency. But finding a balance between planning and improvising is the only way to protect oneself long term from the Systemic Inertia that Operational Excellence naturally leads to.

"Our innovation programs always run on schedule" - person always ignoring unexpected & better ideas.

Innovation is 50% what you can do and 50% what you can get away with.

Delays imply quality issues as much as planning issues.

When things suddenly change, just hold on tight rather than try correcting it immediately – it could well just be turbulence.

The trouble with surprises is that they're unexpected. Particularly the ones you hadn't planned for.

The most popular idea is not necessarily the best one. Although that all depends on whether you're talking before or after launch.

Domain names are the new trademarks, but better.

If Operational Excellence and efficient use of resources were truly important, Heathrow and Gatwick would be the most reliable airports in the world.

Funny how quality stuff is worth maintaining whilst it's the crappy stuff that actually needs it.

Great prototypes are held together by duct tape and magic, poor ones by MS Project.

If things are not working out as planned, you may well have spent too much time planning.

Is there a system or procedure for inventing new systems and procedures?

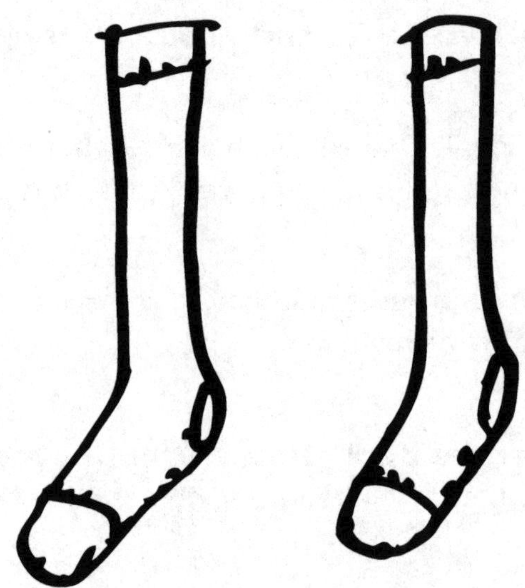

A SPARE PAIR OF LUCKY SOCKS DOES NOT COUNT AS PLAN B

Funny how videoconferencing involves a lot more waving than any other type of meeting.

There is no such thing as 'unbalanced'. Only things that are balanced unfavourably to where you'd like them to be.

Of course, one possible explanation might be there is no explanation.

[I hear it takes about five years to become an overnight success.]

Pondering over two alternatives is just your conscious mind trying to convince your subconscious mind to reconsider.

That fact something is very unlikely doesn't mean it won't happen. Just like someone always wins the lottery, it's just unlikely to be you.

"Tried and Tested" methods are what one reaches for when in panic. Even when they've been proven to fail over and over. Habits die hard.

When asking yourself 'Is it feasible?' the key is understanding that it's as much about working on the 'it' as on the 'feasible'.

The devil is in the detail. Luckily, the divine is too.

In hindsight everything is obvious, including the inconceivable and the impossible.

Problems keep you occupied, solutions even more so.

Cutting costs is not a strategy, but being the cheapest is.

If new ideas required processes to be conceived, JFK would have said "before the end of the decade we will have NASA", not "a man on the moon".

Your market share growing from 90% to 91% may feel puny, but for the other player that meant 10% to 9% which has 10x the relative impact.

If gross margin were really as important as you think it is, your competitors wouldn't make you as nervous as you know you are.

Just like you avoid certain people because they kill your new ideas – they're avoiding you because you always congest their streamlined processes.

Value is remembered long after the price has been forgotten.

"Quick & Dirty Solution" - Funny how only the middle word carries any truth. Which is more than "Temporary Solution", where neither is true.

Growing pains - the fact you know it'll happen doesn't make it any less painful when you're in the middle of it. Like childbirth, probably.

Don't delude yourself into thinking you're discussing *what* you're going to do, when you're only talking about *how* you'll do it.

Paranoia, secrecy and speed to market are many times more effective than any patent can ever be.

YES MA'AM, I KNOW YOU PUT OUT THE FIRE. I JUST WANT TO MAKE SURE IT YOU DID IT ACCORDING TO DIN4102-22.

Calculating ROI on a one sentence concept is like suggesting to get married on a first date: in some cultures it's perfectly acceptable.

The simplest problems can spin out of control if you take time to think about them.

Hey marketing managers: When did you last consider your factories an asset, rather than an obstacle?

Airport security must be the only place in the world where "oh just randomly" is considered a good reason for doing something.

Don't mistake “potential” for “value”, they're on different time lines.

Hey, if you don't like the way we run this metro, go take one in another town.

Of course, once it's perfect, it still needs a lot of improvement.

Innovation success levels are best raised by raising caffeine levels first.

Whatever your MBA mind may tell you, in innovation a straight line is much less effective than a meandering one.

As long as the majority of the Western world calls vegetables "rabbit food" there's no chance of us all living to be 100.

Ambiguity doesn't fare well in an operational world, but a creative context, I'm afraid it's essential.

“2 + 2 = 4”, regardless of culture, religion or political stance. But it does assume you've agreed using a base-10 counting protocol.

Versatile and Efficient are mutually exclusive. Whatever the business book promises, you can't excel at both.

Fancy hotel rooms - there's always one light you can't find the switch for.

Any debate as to where 'breaking point' lies is hypothetical until it actually breaks. Before then, it's mere emotions in conversation.

Breakthrough graphic design drives trial, not repeat. Breakthrough product design drives repeat, not trial. So you still need to do both.

Don't call things "barriers" just because you haven't done them before.

Don't walk into anything you can't walk away from. That goes for cave exploration, Sao Paulo by night and procurement negotiations.

ERP, MRP, systems & procedures automation: the different types of databases available to structure your countless Excel sheets.

If you're not complaining about the pain in the arse that innovation is most of the time, you're not innovating properly.

"As seen on TV" - just so you know, because you probably didn't see it.

Insisting on having breakthrough ideas AND a fixed development budget is like insisting on having kids AND French nails.

If you want people to smile when hearing of your new product, consider naming it the TinkyWillyStrudel instead of the RX2000i.

Hey experts - are you merely distinguishing the insane from the feasible or are you making the insane feasible?

In some categories, retail price is still defined by cost of materials. What do you call one notch below "commodity"?

"Extended Offer!!" - sells poorly, even at reduced price

It seems the phrase "more likely than not" is too often interpreted as "100% definitely yes". At least more often than not.

Modern cars are ultra-safe for crash test dummies. Yet people still get killed. Your model is not reality.

Competitors under-pricing you, use their profits to increase quality. Which gives you TWO problems, not one.

It's all about the deatils.

If you innovate your way into trouble, you need good operational skills to get out. And vice versa.

Whatever factory you visit, regardless of what they produce, always compliment the floor manager on his/her choice of raw materials.

"August 12th. Great, it's almost Christmas." – half of all retail teams, anywhere.

If anyone objects to, or doubts the quality of your big new idea... distract them by starting a hair-splitting discussion on the meaning of the word "innovation".

If you've come to present the outcomes of a project, no one's eager to hear all about the process first.

REMARKABLY, THE REAL THING IS NO WHERE NEAR AS BAD AS IT IS ON PAPER.

How come Planning Meetings always overrun?

More advertising for a failing product is like speaking louder to a person who speaks another language, hoping to be understood.

Like children, ideas will eventually grow up and walk out into the world on their own. But not before having gone through puberty with you.

"There are 7 fundamental ways of organizing a business. Yet over 50% of the companies out there don't follow any of them" - Idiot with an MBA.

Step 1 to bringing down product cost is cranking up volume, not finding cheaper parts.

If you're spending more time honing the pre-amble than the idea, don't even try launching it. Find another place to work.

[**The money your consumer saved from that discount you gave will be spent on something else that isn't discounted – not on you.**]

Countries that shut down in August work 1/12th harder the rest of the year, right?

Some rooms are cool, good for meetings. Other rooms are hot, good for Bikram Yoga. The two are not compatible.

"Deja Due" - the illusion of having missed a deadline before it's actually passed.

Always check before using a file labelled 'Final' by colleagues. There may well be one labelled 'Final4' or 'FinalReleased' out there too.

Just because it looks good in Excel doesn't mean it's good in the real world.

Successful new products and services are a bit like the weather; about 70% identical to yesterday's products.

There's no point debating your portfolio strategy if you have only one product. Seriously.

Remember back when stuff only looked good on paper, you at least had some paper? Now It's only looking good on *.pptx, if you're lucky.

Product launch is not the endpoint of an innovation process. It's at best the halfway point.

Things that are difficult to dispose of: nuclear waste, conscience, children, reputation, dreams, CO2, MRSA and childhood Lego.

"Western population is growing fatter and fatter" - finally some good news for our ailing pension funds.

When you introduce an innovative process, at least reserve some budget for the poor guy/gal who has to rewrite all your ISO9001 certificates.

Corporate ideation birth chambers are, like any birth chamber, quite messy.

So your ISO9001 procedure describes innovation as a yearly workshop with a madman in a Hawaiian shirt shouting 'great idea' all day long?

Visibility on shelf is important, indeed. But not as important as being visible in the place your product is supposed to be used.

"Buy One, Get One Free" - our sales KPIs are on volume, not margin. And we don't have a clue what you'd pay full price for.

[The difference between running projects and ruining projects can be as little as a 1-letter typo.]

Then again, the unsung benefit of a totally miserable innovation process is that everyone will want to get over with it quickly.

The Chicago L track... Certainly someone must have interrupted the structural design phase asking: "Are we all sure steel isn't too noisy?"

I would like to suggest using broccoli to coat the next generation of orbit & re-entry space shuttles. Nothing cools faster than broccoli.

THE PLANT
6σ OFFICES

A webcam adds 10 pounds. So there's some innovation necessary before women will allow video conferencing to become the new standard.

Only few things explode when the pressure rises too high. Most things just crack and start leaking. Sorry, I meant humans.

"Now 30% off" – now 0% off, but we think you won't notice.

The price is almost never too high. It's usually the value which is too low.

Note that the people who populate the Gantt charts confuse "check promising alternative" with "delay". Don't even try to explain.

Whatever manufacturing principle you're considering, there's only a very thin line between lean & mean and malnourished.

The secret to tracking less noise & error is tracking less.

"Limited Offer" - one warehouse full to be precise and we're never ever going to run a batch of this disaster product again.

If you need to update your MS Project Gantts daily, you are not planning. You're merely recording the past - and wasting your time.

Whether or not it's a comeback depends on where you peg the reference point. But 20% gain after a 60% drop is *never* a comeback.

Contracts and signed agreements: if they are written properly, they stay tucked away in the drawer forever.

Don't plan prototypes through your MRP system. Unless it can handle a Bill Of Material with only two parts, duct tape and magic.

The Cost-of-Goods delusion. Cheaper ingredients lead to lower quality leads to lower volume leads to higher cost. Higher volume lowers cost.

Wishful thinking is fine, up to the moment that reality presents itself.

Measuring and controlling are too often confused as meaning the same.

That fact it appears disorganised doesn't automatically mean it is inefficient or unproductive.

Has your Lean/6σ VP suggested ways to make his/her own team obsolete yet? I thought so.

"The Schmeeting Point" - the point when more time is spent in meetings discussing what to do, than the time spent doing what is discussed.

Is there a process for being result-focused?

Step 1 in improving efficiency is building trust, not process control. Simply because it allows you to scrap meetings and reviews.

"Who would like to join our committee to discuss ways of reducing non-value-add operational projects and processes?"

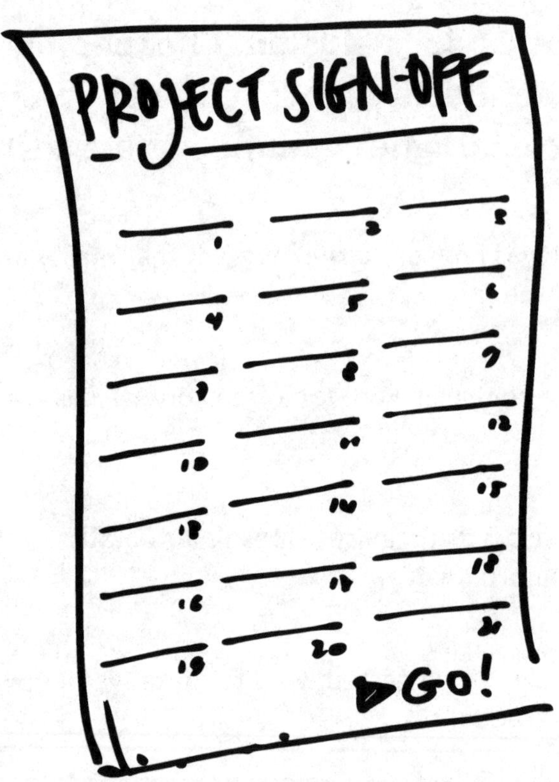

Breakthrough innovation is about resolving category barriers, not your own manufacturing limitations.

Failure Mode & Effect Analysis overviews tend to cover technology assessment only. I bet FMEA's were invented by a commercial team. #Irony

Don't change a winning formula? My impression is winning formulas contain less and less formula over time.

Process efficiency implies *less* process, not more.

Dear Operational Excellence manager, there's no point boasting improved asset efficiency if the excess capacity isn't used making something else.

An innovation process that has become part of your operational structure is as flawed as an operational process that is re-invented continuously.

[Nothing is impossible.
It's just that some things are bloody expensive.]

Feasibility issues? You mean CapEx and Cost Of Goods issues. Which you should have dealt with up front.

Shipping more air with your new 'mousse' food product to save cost? Why not go all the way? Inflate it at shelf and save on logistics too.

Don't be fooled by political barriers being presented as technical barriers.

If you only have a clipper, every problem seems like a nail.

Market Research & Modelling Madness

HONESTLY? I THINK IT TASTES LIKE DOG'S TESTICLES. BUT I'M SURE IT'S WHAT CONSUMERS WANT BECAUSE WE CO-CREATED IT WITH 15,000 OF THEM ACROSS 12 MARKETS.

Market Research & Modelling Madness

Corporate market research is mostly a rational process, whilst people are mostly emotionally driven. That discrepancy exists because people may well act on whims, but you can't run a business on whims. At least not officially.

Hence 'market knowledge' comes in the rational form of market research departments that feed market & consumer data into the other parts of the business. Statisticians with huge brains populate this area, applying big mathematics and promising us true understanding of what's going on in the big bad world outside the company walls. They can show what rational and emotional drivers are making your market happen. It's like having an oracle in your back room and it can be all too tempting to let the data make the decisions for you instead of merely informing them.

When you operate in mass markets, it is in practice impossible to talk to all of your potential 1×10^x ($x>>3$) customers. The business needs prompt and cheap access to answers – particularly in fast moving, competitive environments. Luckily, statisticians offer us shortcuts: *samples*. If you just ask a few hundred people for an opinion, their answers will be representative for the opinions of the whole population.

Not.

- ***Research data is skewed.*** *People have ninja level skills when it comes to sneaking past research recruiters. Whether it's clipboard guys in supermarkets, call centres or online surveys, the feedback they collect is skewed towards the part of the population too polite to say "sorry – I'm not interested".*

- ***Joe Average may not have much to say.*** *In the context of innovation, querying average consumers will get you average answers. Even heavy users don't necessarily engage with their* *products. The fact you run your dishwasher twice a day doesn't mean you have anything interesting to say about dishwasher tablets. Of course there are people out there with profound, avant-garde views on dishwashing – but they're not average and they don't live in typical research panels.*

Receiving answers to questions doesn't mean you're asking the right questions. *We all love asking lotsa questions, it gives us mortals a sense of getting closer to the truth. But curious researchers often overlook that real people simply don't know all the details the researcher would love to uncover. They remember incorrectly if they had two beers with their spaghetti Bolognese last month or three colas with their hamburger. But most people are nice, gentle souls and they'll give you an answer either way. And they'll do so even quicker after 30 minutes of ploughing through a tedious survey.*

Developed to 'test well'. *Probably the biggest problem of follows from all of the above: the tendency of research to be institutionalized in tollgate decision making. Rather than removing the risk of launching the wrong products, it leads to a mind-set of creating propositions that do well in tests rather than in market. Endless honing and word-smithing of identical concepts just to get them to score above go/no-go thresholds instead of picking the right direction from a batch of distinguishable alternatives.*

t all hopeless and is market research useless? Of course not. Keep mind this is not about day-to-day operational stuff, like measuring e efficacy of a commercial or how well you're doing in comparison a competitor. The context I'm describing is that of *innovation*, a zzy world with far less clarity for respondents to hold on to, simply cause they're being asked to comment about products that do t yet exist. Even the most elaborate concept description and age storyboard will require a respondent to *imagine* what it's like use the product or service. That's difficult. This means the normal tistical rules around sampling do not apply, human error sits in the way too much. One cannot ask even the savviest consumer to rank a feeling of "Dunno, maybe I'd try" on a 5-point Lickert scale and expect an accurate response. Nor will refining the options to a 10-point scale make the outcome any more precise, no matter what maths you unleash upon it.

Then what to do with research for innovation? Face-to-face qualitative research can only carry so far; there will come a moment you and your colleagues at risk management will want some cover from bigger numbers.

- ***Talk to the right people****. Once you've realized most respondent panels are skewed, you may as well bend it in your favour. Filter for the category Lead Users [von Hippel 1986]. About 5-10% of any category's consumers show a significantly higher interest for improvements from that category. They're frustrated, try and tinker with product variations and simply have a much deeper need for progress from brands and companies like yours. They're almost always one step ahead of the masses' category behaviour, just what you need. But be aware this is category-led and not personality-led. Lead users have more interest in a few categories, not all of them. I'm a lead user of yoghurts myself, but couldn't care less about custards.*

- ***Be comfortable with being ROUGHLY right****. Just like censorship is often self-applied, most precision is demanded by people doing their own measurements. Moving in the right direction is much more valuable than spending forever trying to precisely measure something that does not yet exist. And because you keep moving, you can enjoy the relaxedness of doing sequential batches of small research rather than one big budget-guzzling piece that has the future of the business – or at least your career – depending on it.*

- ***Forget about early adopters****. These people tend to be mere shopaholics and everyone who buys a lot will get lucky and be 'on trend' more often than normal mortals.*

- ***Stay away from brand lovers.*** *Once they've calmed down from the excitement that someone working for their favourite brand is asking them questions, they aren't very likely to give you valuable critique as to what you're up to for future launches. Would you offer valuable feedback to someone you are madly in love with?*

- ***Be cautious with generalizations.*** *Someone once pointed me to the fact the average consumer has one tit and one testicle. Statistically 100% true – and 100% useless. To get insight into the lives and drivers of millions of people, a degree of generalization will always be necessary. Using consumer 'personas' is an example of using such shortcuts, but they can lead down a tricky path. Not because the underlying statistics aren't sound, but because personas tend to become a catch-all for very elementary human drivers (think Maslow) without relevant context of a particular situation. And it's those situational settings that provide the best base for creating innovative products. With only personas and their abstract motivations to go on, context will be extrapolated on the spot – "Oh, I think Helga The Hunter-Gatherer would really love this". And then we're in fantasy land.*

Paraphrasing the brilliant philosopher Alfred Korzibsky:

Your model ...

... is NOT reality.

No matter how much love and care you put into creating it, no matter how great it would be if the model were 100% accurate, it never is. In the context of innovation, trust your model only to inform your decisions but *never* let it make the decisions for you.

Speaking of male chauvinism, the pilot on my flight home was a real character. She said we all think in stereotypes.

Opinions will do just fine as long as the truth is unclear. Just don't confuse the two, please.

Beware of the mischievous bell curve, its tails are fatter than you think. And it may be more pointy. Actually it may not be bell shaped at all.

"Wisdom of crowds"? On average, everyone in the hippodrome loses at the races. "Wisdom of the bookies" is a better inspiration for strategy.

Would you have rated a high Purchase Intent score for all the kitchen appliances (men) and shoes (women) you have in the house? Be honest.

"And that, my friends, is the truth" - market researcher's famous last words

A 2nd opinion is just that: an opinion. You choose what your truth will be. How very metaphysical.

"We're doing our very best to help stranded passengers with food, drink and free WiFi" - Maslow needs revision.

Keep in mind that consumer drivers in the UK and Japan drive on the wrong side of the road.

Confidence driven by facts and confidence driven by statistics are not the same. But you can pretend it is, as no one seems to have noticed this yet.

Knowing the n=150 fish in your aquarium really well doesn't mean you can predict fish behaviour in all of the Atlantic.

Try completing one of your own surveys first before complaining about drop-out rates.

The more you interpret the data, the further you dwell from the truth, by definition. Your beautiful map is not reality.

When creating a need segmentation study, please segment along customer needs or occasions. Not along your company's organizational chart.

'Science' means looking for falsification, not more proof you're right.

With obesity and poverty expanding globally at the rates they do... isn't predicting today's new-borns will all live to be 100 rather naive?

If you're struggling to uncover clear needs, cast a narrower net. It's easier finding bankable kitchen needs than home needs than life needs.

Remember the days when "the data" would answer your business questions for you?

HEY, DON'T SNEAK UP ON ME LIKE THAT, WILL YA?

Ask yourself: 'revealed' versus 'declared' consumer behaviour... Which is best at uncovering opportunities and which are you using now?

By definition, the population sample that's representative for your next opportunity is not representative for the current status quo.

Opportunities without risk only exist in the past. If you see a future opportunity without risk, brace yourself for surprises.

Topping the menu in most bars is their free WiFi, not their food & drink. Just like my ISP offers coupons for pizza delivery deals.

When creating a vision, emphasis on market research will ensure your case is history-proof, not future-proof.

Trendspotting and trainspotting have a lot more in common than just the binoculars, cameras, newsletters, clipboards and eleven letters.

If you knew what to look for, you wouldn't need to look. At least make sure to know why you're looking before worrying where to look.

Keep in mind that historical benchmarks are exactly that: historical. They predict concept performance in case you launched last year.

Not understanding your consumer's motivations is a mutual experience. He/she thinks you're odd too.

If you're looking for experts on near future developments, talk to a bookie. Unlike market researchers, their livelihood depends on correct predictions.

Statistical outliers... maybe it's important, maybe it's a fat finger, maybe it's someone joking around with the clipboard guy.

IF YOU DON'T LIKE MY TRENDS – I HAVE MORE WHERE THESE CAME FROM!

Privacy is like health, you don't really miss until it you lose it. Teenagers care equally little about both.

Sending out ever more surveys to raise confidence usually means distributing them amongst ever less ideal respondents.

Trend watching... The poor man's trend setting.

If your futurologist is surprised you called, find a better one.

Continental drift is a highly predictable macro trend, but quite tough to use as inspiration for new concepts.

Empathy for your consumers doesn't mean that if you like a concept they automatically will too.

Hey market researchers: don't worry about finding the truth. In the end it will find you.

Market Research is a great for predicting the past.

Segmentation 'personas' all too often sound like stereotypes from a cheesy TV sitcom. Which explains the cliché results generated by using them.

The more you need an answer, the fewer questions you ask. And vice versa.

An opinion carried by crowds does not make it more correct. Unless they're also carrying pitchforks and torches.

“4 in 5 market research studies are pretty much useless”, says 1 in 5 market researchers.

A 2% difference in scores between only two concepts means respondents:
A- are deeply polarized
B- can't see the difference
C- don't care.

It cannot be a coincidence that 'quantitative market research' anagrams to 'heart attack via requirements'.

When futurologists say 'because'... be very cautious. When historians say 'because', be even more sceptical.

Clues proving you cannot be wrong are much stronger than those showing you're right.

Funny how the extrapolated extension of 'truth' is 'insight', whereas the extrapolated appendix of 'lies' is 'statistics'.

Whoever feels stuck with abstract personas as target consumer descriptions, ought to come to the IKEA canteen. Everyone 'real' is here.

AND FINALLY, AFTER THREE HOURS OF INTERVIEWING, THE RESPONDENT SAID SHE JUST WANTED THE OLD MODELTO BE CHEAPER.

AND THEN I KILLED HER, YOUR HONOR.

Whenever a futurologist or trend analyst defends past predictions with a sentence starting "if it weren't for...", walk away.

If you're handing out incentives to respondents for any answer they give, why not award prizes for the right answer?

Yo Momma innovates so bad, she brought her own sample to the market research team, in a cup.

Correlation and Causation only differ when you care enough about the topic.

"This morning in the supermarket, I had 72% intent to purchase this product" - no one, ever.

Hey market researchers, enough with the fancy tools OK? Great painters aren't admired for their brushes either. Well, except Bob Ross maybe.

Which one of your trademarked personas are you yourself? Let me guess, you're a mix of at least three of them?

Robo-moderator algorithm: ECHO("Tell me about (Topic$)") THEN LOOP(3;"Why do you say that" OR "tell me more") THEN RANDOM("rank this"; END).

Depending on paid respondents for market research is like walking into a red light district to find true love. Real, but not authentic.

Whomever got the Dualit toaster through concept testing and prototyping deserves the World Spin Award.

How innovative! This focus group facility has doubled the viewing room behind the mirror for use as a sauna!

YoMomma's so fat she skews every sample she ends up in.

Unlike reading reports, you can have new ideas while you sleep. Now who's being efficient, eh?

Some topics simply cannot be made into a science, no matter how badly you want to sound scientific. No control group? No science.

Paraphrasing Mother Theresa: "If I research the masses, I'm paralyzed by pie-charts. If I listen to individuals, I'm inspired to innovate".

Testing a concept without its Umfeld on shelf is no different from buying a house without considering the neighbourhood.

$(TREND)^2$ = the habit of trend watchers to parrot other trend watchers instead of observing populations.

Yo Momma's so bad at market research she thought a respondent pool was for people wearing Speedos and swimming goggles.

Research the idea until the risk has gone and you'll find the opportunity has disappeared along with it.

HOW ODD – ACCORDING TO YOUR DEMOGRAPHIC PROFILES YOU SHOULD HAVE THOUGHT THAT WAS INCREDIBLY FUNNY.

Only in market research are we happy to take advice from total strangers.

I think the best way to moderate a focus group is to pretend you're Oprah Winfrey for 2x 45 minutes.

It's not the volume of data that counts, but the amount of sleep you get to process the little bit of important data.

Funnelvision: If the focus group doesn't like your idea, re-recruit and re-test 'till it passes.

Offering multiple choice answers is a sign you don't know what question to ask.

We found a way to measure 100% accurate Purchase Intent and it involves baby unicorns.

* SPOILER ALERT * A USP in no way guarantees actual selling.

I am at this very moment experiencing a very niche consumer need for on-the-go stain remover. In particular for molten Mozzarella stains.

If you ask lapsed users why they left, OF COURSE they will say it was because of price. They're too nice to tell you the truth.

Be smart in a downward economy and halve your market research recruitment costs through respondents with split personality disorder.

Somewhere, a marketing manager is planning new products based on a persona just like you.

Input: 24x observations, 8x opinionated session participants and 46x verbatim, How many insight permutations does that lead to?

Did you do your due diligence and check with consumers or did you check with consumers to do your due diligence? – Not the same.

THOSE OUTLIERS ARE MAKING ME NERVOUS TOO, BUT I SUGGEST WE IGNORE THEM JUST FOR NOW, OK?

How many of the consumers from your last co-creation session would you hire as Product Development Manager? Then use their input accordingly.

YoMomma's so fat she can make n=1 volumetric modeling credible.

You can predict next year's trends with 90% accuracy by copying last year's trends. Which shows how 90% accurate can be 100% useless.

"Cleaning the Data", aka "Censoring".

Why use the Large Hadron Collider? I know market research departments creating datasets large enough to reveal the Higgs Boson every week.

People are even lazier than they are vain.

When was the last time you did a reality-check on your Excel-sheet driven strategy? And quant research doesn't count as 'reality'.

[**Don’t mix statistics with catch-all terminology. "62.4% want Eco-friendly products" doesn't mean ANYthing.**]

Statistically, there's no difference between you throwing the dice or a stranger doing it for you. Now tell me you’re not superstitious and let me throw for you.

Yo Momma's so fat, she's her own mass market.

When people speak of 'dynamic' lifestyles, they often mean the opposite: 'turbulent'. An active way of standing still.

There are two types of people; those who leave OEM stickers all over their laptops and cameras, and those who don't understand these people.

[In the simplified reality of market research, the difference between good and bad is merely a question of benchmarks.]

Somewhere, the folks marketing products you love, talk about you & your habits with the same simpleton tone you talk about your consumers.

Decision making: when entering new terrain, a compass will outperform any map. Particularly one created behind a desk.

"Significance levels? The Consumer Truth? What I'm revealing here is your FATE!" - balsy market researcher pushing the envelope.

A market research report presented as a story is very compelling. But remember the ugly reality has no plot, no narrative, no climax, no ending.

"So if everyone starts jumping off a cliff, you'd do too then?!"
- If your parent is a trend watcher, the answer they want to hear is "Yes".

It seems modern market research machismo all boils down to who has the biggest data.

"Concept Screening" anagrams to "Connecting Creeps" - remember, you heard it here first.

Yo Momma's so fat, analysts call her when they need Big Data.

Ask a consumer for an opinion and they'll give you one. Not because they have an opinion, but because you asked for one.

[Trend reports are like weather reports, sending everyone to the same, overcrowded sunny beaches. Real value is spotting the rain ahead.]

I hear Neuro MR is so expensive it sits in the CFO's budget.

If numerologists can 'predict' Kennedy's murder from the Bible, imagine the nonsense you can 'mine' from 1.7Tb of consumer data.

You'll have to accept - and defend - that "maybe" is sometimes the best possible answer.

Re-framing 'stereotyping' as 'segmentation study' must be the market research industry's greatest PR stunt to date.

The middle word in "insight" is "sigh".

If alien civilizations would read a typical FMCG research report, their first conclusion would be humans stop buying stuff at the age of 49.

Best-Sellers, Fiction, Non-Fiction, Business, Science, Children and Self-Help. The sections in a typical FMCG segmentation study report.

[The best crystal balls don't look into the future, but selectively regurgitate stuff from the past.]

Great project prank to mess up your colleague's concept scores: add "with free coupons" to the worst concept's benefit statement.

"I don't know" - is a message seldom delivered with the clarity it deserves.

Big Data isn't new. Just check pages 3 to 467 of your reasearch report. It's all there.

I wonder if religious people see the irony of most atheists ALSO completely mixing up causation and correlation.

Statistical significance vs financial significance: when market research is SO expensive that the outcomes simply have to be true.

[Unless you work in office furniture design, there's little chance you do decent consumer research sitting at your desk.]

NO, I DON'T GET IT. YOU SAID YOU WANTED A POOL OF RESPONDENTS.

Yo Momma's so fat she's a heavy user in every category.

* SPOILER ALERT * The €500K segmentation study you just commissioned will reveal an axis labelled ME-WE and claim that is very relevant.

Yesterday I had a vodka; then wrote three concepts and filed my taxes. The concepts bombed but my tax man scored top-2 purchase intent.

I have a hunch that SPSS was originally coded by Uri Geller. And then debugged by Houdini.

Just like gold mining, data mining unearths mostly gravel and fossils.

"I understand you're not comfy in that MRI scanner and you'd rather go home, but this is costing us $60K a day so shut up" - Neuro MR

Statistical analysis is about interpreting what you observed, not bridging the gap to what you hoped were true & think is right.

"Tell me a little more... WHY should I take the garbage out?" - focus group moderator heading for trouble by taking work behaviours home.

FACT: Beware of trend spotters talking about 'facts'.

If you diligently dig through all 380 pages of a typical quant research report, you'll eventually reach the arse it was meant to cover.

"CONFESS!! NOW TALK, YOU B*STARD!!" - market researcher interrogating the data.

When you're desperate for good news, n=1 is suddenly good enough.

[What's more convincing? A market researcher with a PhD or one who has QUAL & QUANT tattooed on his knuckles?]

Paradox: 'laziness' is a consumer driver.

Sometimes focus group outputs are so spot on strategy, you'd wonder if the mirror wasn't mounted the wrong way around.

If you layer 3 consumer frameworks on top of each other, you'll never need to talk to a real person again to make your Excel forecast work.

Brand managers talking about loving their consumers - it says more about their perception of love than of their relationship with consumers.

We needed idiot-proof concepts, so we ran a co-creation session with a bunch of statistically representative idiots.

"Co-creation? Man, never again" - Adam, rubbing his sore ribs.

Market research is not meant to reduce risk, but to navigate it. To help & support your decisions, not to make them for you.

Remember that only the summary slide of your 423 page report will survive and lead a life of its own. The reasoning will vanish.

"... And to really get to the bottom of it, we need to do more market research." - the final sentence of 99% of market research reports.

Decision Making Along The S-Curve

YOUR OTHER IDEAS WERE ALL CULLED IN ACCORDANCE TO MY KPI'S.

Decision Making Along The S-Curve

Dynamic systems – be it people, businesses or products – evolve roughly according to an S-curve.

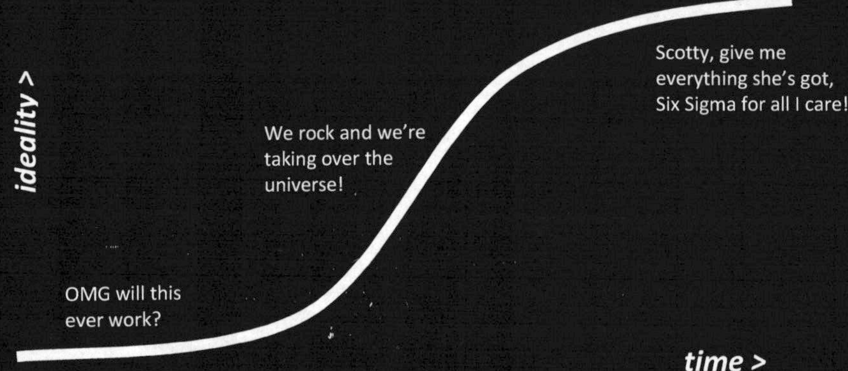

This flow across three main stages (infancy, growth, maturity) has been common understanding for at least half a century, probably much longer. And here's a funny thing I noticed whilst searching for representations of S-curves online:

A) When they're used to describe *business* growth, they're usually stacked like this:

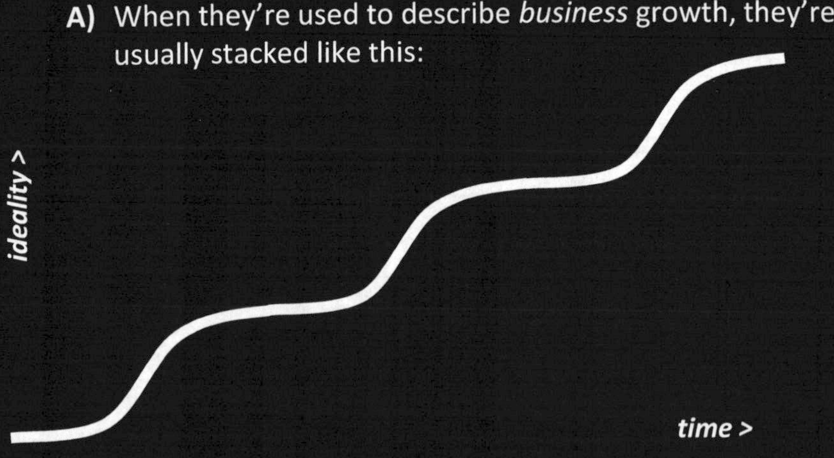

B) But when describing *technology* evolution, they are stacked quite differently:

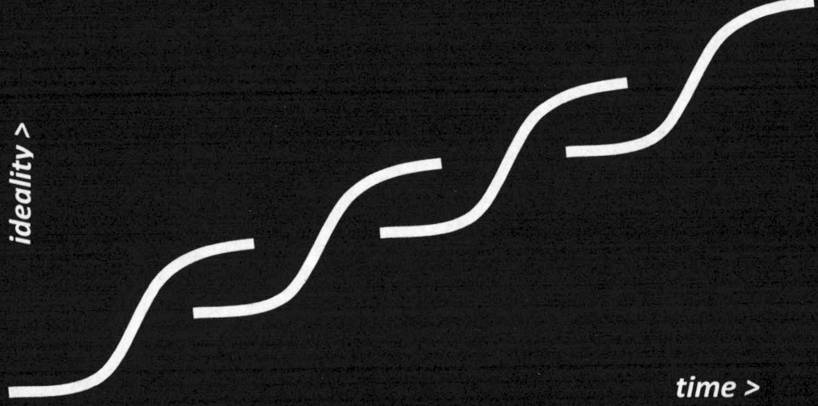

The difference is obviously the way they connect. **A)** is all about good news, whilst **B)** shows that whatever new curve kicks off, there will be a lapse in ideality (=efficiency) when you transition.

In case you're wondering, **B)** is the correct one. Libraries could be filled with case studies of companies sliding into oblivion because they couldn't switch to the new technology for no other reason than it would kill their short term profitability along with their cash cow. This is why game changers are *almost* never introduced by market leaders. When they do, it requires an existential crisis.

Which brings us to the topic of decision making. Taking a truly grumpy view on this, we can assume that human decisions will always be made with the best interest of that particular Human in mind. In a business environment with a proper hierarchy in place, this is then less about decisions and more about offering scenarios to the next person upstream that will make the Human look good:

- ***High reward.*** *Acting in best interest of the business, generating growth, everyone achieves their KPI's.*

- ***Low risk.*** *Doing the above with least risk, resource or cost within the period the Human is expected to be in his/her current role.*

With this perception of human nature in mind, it's pretty obvious that ignorance or denial of what the next evolutionary phase holds in store will lead to 'good news' - and a severly blinkered view on what scenarios are best for the business.

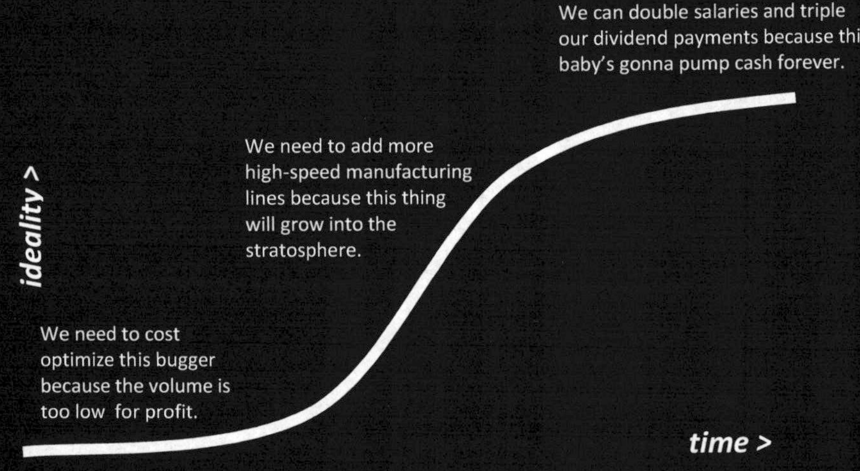

Is this too harsh? Is this just another plea for longer term KPI's and rewards for management? Partially. For an innovative corporate culture to grow sustainably, it must reward decisions that ensure the business is future-proof, because business reality will have changed by the time scenarios trickle down into action:

- *When your expensive, rattling prototypes show promise they might actually work: start building them in a low-volume and flexible pilot setup rather than waiting for the perfection necessary to produce them on expensive high-speed assets.*
- *When recruiting new team members, assume the business will have evolved and grown by the time they're in place.*
- *When production capacity starts to max out, don't simply install a copy of your existing manufacturing line but build one you can more easily re-tool for the next generation when demand goes down again – which it will.*

Setting KPI's to entice such future-proofing mean they should reward not what would be great *now*, but what would facilitate evolving to the next phase of your business. None of this is rocket science, yet it seems a struggle for small and large businesses alike.

It's no different from raising children. You don't buy clothes that fit snugly now, you buy things they will grow into soon. You look ahead, because you *know* they'll grow.

What this boils down to?

Planning for success ...

... is planning for transition.

1853, Elisha Otis. I wonder where he pitched his idea for the elevator.

Most decision makers need to see a few options first, before they can say "no".

Show me five good reasons not to progress a new idea and I'll show you at least ten better ones.

The pyramids weren't built top-down either.

If you're hoping for things to get better, they will definitely get worse first. Hope is not a strategy.

It's a shame you can't recover the black box after a failed market launch.

The guys on the other side of the fence are busy genetically engineering greener grass right now.

When you're confronted with a stunning competitive market introduction, "how did they do that?" is the least of your worries.

Once you've achieved "perfection", the next stage is "promising alternative".

Live like there's no tomorrow - a guarantee to remain stuck in yesterday.

I wonder what happens when this tsunami of Y-Gens suddenly all realize they're not geniuses and just as mediocre as us X-Gens before them?

Any idea is only as good as the length of time to find a better one. Hopefully it'll be yours again.

You can't blame the other person for being tolerated.

[Most business books on succeeding in innovation forget to mention "willingness to work Saturdays and Sundays".]

Funny things happen when young marketing managers take over a brand and aren't aware what part of the brand history was truth and what was spin.

Bigger and Badder: If your EPD threshold is being just about acceptable in comparison to last year's EPD, you'll end up with a shitty product.

Only Generation-Y truly understand the importance of Lady Gaga as a cultural phenomenon. Only Generation-X understand both need to grow up.

"Get straight to the periphery of the problem" seems to be the preferred approach in today's innovation teams.

If you're wondering what innovation to launch next, just ask yourself what would be your worst nightmare for a competitor to launch.

Head in the sand or head in the clouds, both make you neck hurt.

Pushing new ideas through an organization: the pain is definitely real. Shame that the cause usually isn't.

Best way to learn implementing breakthrough innovation: implement not-so-breakthrough innovation first and see where the system pushes back.

When was it that we all started assuming there's a simple solution to every problem, regardless of its complexity?

On your quest for the person who can say 'yes' to your idea, you'll meet many who can say 'no' first. Make friends to make it happen.

For innovators with a large sophisticated toolbox, every problem becomes a complex multi-disciplinary challenge. Sometimes hammers are good.

"Yes, of course your innovation program will throw up a hurdle. Now stop whining and get over it".

Decision making on gut instinct may save us time and the bore of post-rationalization, but it doesn't mean it's less prone to error.

When weighing pro's and con's, be aware that the con's are in reality inversed pro's of alternatives you haven't yet considered.

Milestones' and 'Tollgates' are a managerial invention. Reality is fluid.

GRRRRREAT PRODUCT. IS THERE A WAY WE CAN CONNECT IT TO OUR FACEBOOK PAGE?

CONSUMERS LOVE FACEBOOK YOU KNOW.

The typical number of bridges between FMCG Marketing and Manufacturing teams is either none or one too far.

There are always more reasons in favour of holding another meeting than there are for scrapping an existing one. Like with government legislation.

Insisting on first-time-right innovation -without detours- is like urging to paddle when you could be sailing. More tiring and much slower.

Check if your Risk Management Advisor ties double knots in his/her shoelaces. If not, walk away.

Inertia is not an external factor stopping you. Nor is paralysis.

Just like one creates solutions step-by-step and not instantly, one might as well throw up problems one-by-one rather than all at once.

"You're one in a million" sounds so much nicer than "there are only about 6,500 other people just like you".

Innovation decisions: one path takes you to endless hard work, missed holidays and possibly divorce. The other path takes you to failure.

You can't blame poor innovators for the fact they have so many other important meetings to attend.

Urgent, important, critical. Three words meaning entirely different things, yet so often mixed up. Even by smart people.

Stakeholders who have nothing to win/lose are not stakeholders. They're just nosy, bossy or simply bored and they should be kept at distance.

The sun's energy for 1 minute can power the world for a year. Yeah. And all the water in the sea can quench humanity's thirst for eternity.

Balancing 'Time', 'Cost' & 'Quality' in any project is like a game of Whack-The-Mole. Bring in 'Politics' to keep them all above ground.

Big ideas sometimes need to be dressed up as small ones, just to survive company politics and decision making procedures.

Conflicts exist where you choose not to walk away. But walk away too soon and you'll find the conflict comes with you as a moral dilemma.

When two opinions clash, it's usually not the opinions that matter but their owners. Compromises save face, solutions make partners.

Maybe successful innovation really is no more than just doing what everyone else is thinking?

How come time slows down the closer you get to your destination? Unless your destination is a deadline.

Sunday evening is the new Monday morning.

In an ideal world, mistakes have 'rewind' buttons to undo the damage. On the other hand, a crisis needs a 'fast forward'.

The journey from problem to solution can resemble a game of Chinese Whispers. Only without the laughter at the end.

When you're really hungry, even crap food tastes delicious. Same story when you're starving for new ideas. Don't ideate on an empty funnel.

Brand lovers are about as good a judge about the brand as anyone who is head-over-heels in love.

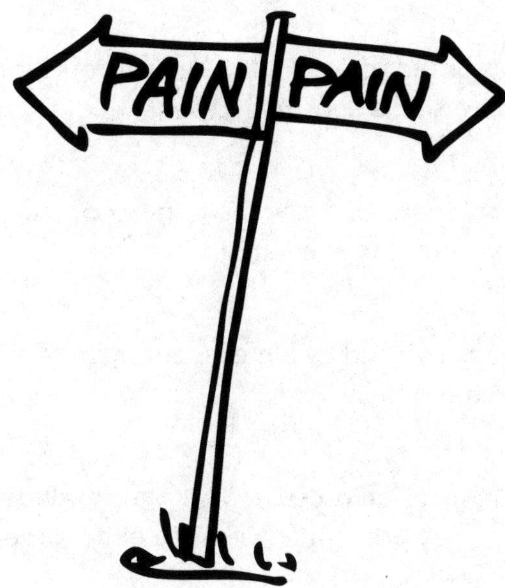

"No, I don't see the irony at all", replied the trend spotter who kept on whining about the current tough market for trend spotting agencies.

Are smartphones making me dumber? They must be.

[When you reach the end of the page in your notebook, it coincidentally always feels like you've made just about enough notes.]

Naivety is one of the most expensive talents to be blessed with.

You can fake workshop energy levels - but you can't fake innovation success.

“I really wish this brand offered me a more diverse, richer portfolio experience” - not a single consumer, ever.

Reminder: you do *not* need twice the number of line extensions on shelf to double your brand's revenue.

If you have to be convinced by a metric that you're successful, then you probably aren't.

Tightly defined innovation processes not only exclude the necessity for getting lucky, they prevent any chance of it happening entirely.

[Whether you bet on Plan A or Plan B - you only ever get Result A.]

Whatever attracted your consumer, will also pull them away. Win on price, lose on price. Ensure your differentiating benefit lasts.

Runaway successes need good shoes, not business planning.

When scoping your project: remember that you, your team, your boss and your boss' bosses are not the people actually buying your product.

Every innovation success story has this moment where the "can we please speed up" attitude switches to "for god sake slow down please".

Innovation is as much about knowing what to ignore as what to follow.

No, most personalities are not layered like onions. More like eggs. Crack the thin civilized shell and the messy insides come running out.

Every innovation team has an Axl Rose who walks out on tedious jobs and a Slash who can't finish his solos.

Corporate navel gazing also involves lots of fluff.

Somewhere, right now, someone's considering advertising their business in a phone book.

You can't buy momentum, sadly. Nor a trend.

Claiming you're "living on the edge" says less about the "edge" and more about what you call "living".

Poor quality coffee makes me really opinionated about just about everything.

Good news always comes in pairs; mostly because the high of the first one influences your judgment for a while. Ditto for bad news.

[If you get no reaction, your action is the problem (Newton's 3rd).]

Compromises eventually catch up with you, being something neither of you wanted.

Is there a way to make a scattered, granular organization work as one harmonious entity (like a beehive) without sounding like a hippie?

Under the right circumstances, a university degree and PhD in molecular science can be trumped by 6 evening classes on PowerPoint skills.

Of course, if the outlook is bleak - you can always indulge in the cocoon of wishful thinking.

If you give something away for free, the money your 'client' saves won't come your way later. It'll go somewhere else that isn't free, now.

It's the simple stuff that is complex to come up with.

It takes two to polarize.

Marketing disasters don't need more marketing to be undone.

SO WHERE DOES THE FARAOH WANT HIS PYRAMID? HE SUGGESTED WE START WITH THIS POINTY BLOCK. QUICK, IT'S HEAVY.

Opportunitanosmia - the inability to smell an opportunity Paradox: Consumers act mostly on whims, but you can't run a business on whims. Or at least you can't publicly acknowledge you do.

The best indicator of your mental age is what fresh snow does to your sense of mobility.

Surprisingly, a holistic approach works only bottom-up, not top-down.

[Regret is merely an internalized "I told you so".]

Somewhere in a shed in China, someone is already making that brilliant product idea you just had. Unless you're Chinese yourself, of course.

If you want your innovative idea to succeed sooner, launch it in New Zealand.

"We need to go to more of these industry conferences & events" - a team on their way to becoming totally average in the industry.

Can someone remind me what the age cohort was that AB Males buy a pasta machine? I think it came just before the home bread baking machine age cohort.

There are few things more fun than disagreeing with people who know what they're talking about.

Often the cure involves making you more ill first. Just like family photos emailed over from home make you more homesick rather than less.

The best dates to meet are the sweet ones that go into a baklava.

Whatever follows the word "objective" tends to be totally subjective.

Productive week huh? OK, but fighting global/regional teams, or any other group of colleagues doesn't count as productive. Think again.

Don't deal with shit by stepping on it.

Brave is the person who lets a promising idea prevail over short term profit. Hence the innovation always happens in the shed next door.

Beware, nutters can bring on an anaphylactic shock.

The best decisions are made based on a night's sleep, not an analyst's report.

Things besides politics you don't want to be fighting in your innovation project: gravity, floods, civil war, E-bola, migraine & nay-sayers.

I once worked with a brand team that were just like The Avengers. The only real difference was that they were all The Hulk.

BE SMART AND HIDE YOUR PROCRASTINATION UNDER A SMILE AND A THICK BLANKET OF QUESTIONS.

Successful innovation starts with actually doing what you were thinking.

Walking into a meeting you feel you cannot walk away from means, by definition, you've walked into a trap.

Unless you're in the business of building passenger aircraft, you really don't need 20 'critical success factors'. Probably 3 will do.

Of course the BRIC economies offer massive potential. Just don't forget the economies you conveniently share a border with.

If you're wondering how to make your "bad news" board presentation more enjoyable, inhale some helium - then pass the balloon around.

When typing a very big message on your very small phone - consider just making the phone-call instead. Your message will be much clearer.

When setting your team's KPIs, don't forget to specify along which axis you're stretching their goals.

A system is perfect only until the moment everyone understands it. From then on, everyone starts abusing it.

Virtual World corporations are complaining that patents are blocking innovation rather than driving it. Welcome to the Real World, children.

Most boutique services are at best canteen services, in clever disguise.

Be aware that email is a miscommunication accelerator.

After all these years, someone just told me of the Sunk Costs Fallacy. Well, I'm certainly not going to switch to using that non-sense now.

Hey solo professionals. Don't call yourself CEO of your company, it makes you look vain and rather silly.

Key to successful innovation is setting priorities and not being distrac

Alcohol and operating heavy machinery go together fine, but only in the right sequence.

If it takes your business 6 months to do something as simple as register a new vendor, how can you think you can launch a new product in 12?

The moment at which a piece of work is considered 'finished' depends more on the hour of the day than the finishing level of the work itself

A: "Hey, no need to be stressed about this"
B: "But what if it all goes wrong?"
A: "Then you won't have wasted your time stressing about it".

**[In case of error – REWIND
Crisis – FAST FORWARD
Own stupidity – STOP
Competitor's stupidity – RECORD
Boredom – PLAY]**

"I don't like their answer, so I'll ask a different question" - the logic behind many endless multi-disciplinary conversations.

The Entrepreneur's Dilemma: sustainable business growth implies/requires decreasing personal relevance. Ego's disguised as glass ceilings.

When working on your breakthrough innovation, don't forget the not-so-early adopters. They want a fun/tasty/useful product too.

[Anticipation beats prediction.]

Successful negotiation is about keeping focus on what you agree on. Not what you disagree on.

A benefit of being able to change course quickly is that it allows you to be wrong quite often too.

Innovation in mature markets is almost always about getting consumers to switch away from something else.

"Forever" equals about 5-6 months, in most business contexts.

"You need a clear ambition and a simple decision making process" - Great, just like Don Quixote.

You're probably your own bottleneck in many more ways than you realise.

[Keep in mind most of your actions are in fact interactions.]

Question: 3-year plans that need re-writing every year should really be named 1-year plans, right?

Your consumers WILL find out what you just did. Yes, you know what I mean.

"Action driven by fear of inaction", aka "Panic"

True innovation led by your R&D and Manufacturing teams flows not from more Process Control, but less: Process Liberation.

Do not underestimate the motivational power of a well-timed pat on the back.

From now on I will refer to "compromises" as "hybrid solutions".

A $1m incentive can bring down a $1bn empire. Decisions are made in the best interest of the decision maker, not the topic of decision.

"But won't this product cannibalise half our portfolio?" - "Yes, definitely. Or would you prefer a competitor to kill your cash cows?"

"Ambition" before "Exploration" before "Idea" before "Planning" before "Success". But only in the orderly world of the dictionary.

[**Lower ranks are applauded for bringing in fresh ideas. Higher ranks are applauded for not stopping them.**]

Corporate innovation paradox: regardless of the improbability of any idea making it to market, a ruthless emphasis on screening out ideas.

An excellent way to wean your customer off the old product onto the new model, is doing it abruptly, unannounced and without mercy.

Board room agreements are about business objectives, the fights are about the personal consequences.

On the long dark journey of getting innovations to market, even the doldrums have doldrums.

Moore's law for accelerating computing power must have a counterpart for humans dumbing down.

Multi-cultural/lingual corporate environments would do good to adopt the universal language of slapstick more often.

Of the nautical analogies used in business, the barnacle would deserve more attention. We all know one.

Don't forget to start work on V2 of your great new idea in parallel with the V1 launch. Because V2 is the one that just might make you money.

Option paralysis has little to do with the options and everything with the paralyzed.

[Don't say your team won't follow up on your instructions until you've tried Kung Fu Briefing.]

Things that speed up meetings and decision making: focused pre-reads, set agendas, action lists & full bladders.

In Foresight, It's All *So* Obvious.

ISN'T IT GREAT YOU'LL SPEND THE REST OF YOUR CAREER WORKING ON THIS PRODUCT?

In Foresight, It's All So Obivous

This is about your bread & butter having become a commodity and you being on your way out of business. This is a bout Pricing having become the only tool you have left to influence your customer's decision making.

When you lose on price, you are in fact experiencing the consequence of something that happened much earlier and you're proba bly in even more trouble than you are aware of. What may appear like a stroke of bad luck could well be the sign of a deeper, more structural problem.

Imagine one of your customers has chosen to switch to a competitor's product, taking a significant chunk of your business away. A chat in the hallway of your company may then well sound like this:

A) Dude, why the long face? What's happening with that big [client] contract I heard you were bidding for?

B) Not good, it's over. I just heard we lost to [competitor]. A damn disgrace after 5 years of good business with [client].

A) What, you mean [competitor]? The amateurs who've been knocking off bad copies of our [product]?

B) Yes, the &*$)$@£ b**tards undercut our proposal by almost 40%. There was no way we could match that.

A) But their quality is appalling! I thought [client] was anal about quality?

B) They were, but not this time.

A) Surely that will get them in trouble, there's no way [competitor] can produce anything close to our standards. Our quality is FAR better, make that GALACTICALLY better than theirs.

B) I know, I know. Of course [client] will be back in six months, but that's still a lot of revenue gone. Not to mention my bonus.

A) Yeah, they'll be back. You just wait 'till they've really experienced the importance of quality when it comes to [product].

Feel free to insert you own favourites for [client], [competitor] and [product]. What has gone so wrong for these poor people? What to do now? Well, depending on who you are (or whom you ask), you may be considering one of the following:

- You're confident [client] will come back soon, so you'll just lower capacity for 6 months, fire some folks and wait.
- You consider manufacturing more efficiently, invest more in Six Sigma, Lean and DFE to get that cost down.
- You'd rather lower your margin to keep the business, it'll never be good enough for the shareholders anyway, so screw 'em.
- You consider lowering your quality standards and simplify your manufacturing process.
- You now have time to improve quality even further, making [client] return sooner.
- You spend the next twelve months planning a hostile takeover of [competitor].
- You put your R&D at work to develop [product]-LIGHT, the cheap alternative.
- You'll take [competitor] to court for infringing copyrights or patents.

There are many more things you could do, the problem is none of them will do you much good unless you start repairing some of the damage done way before you lost this contract. So here's another way of looking at the situation, which highlights your real problem.

Imagine you are now [competitor] and you're celebrating your first win over the industry leader. You proudly stroll through your rickety old factory where you've been knocking off countless copies for years, shaking hands as you go around. What are you going to do with this new revenue stream you've just secured?

- Buy a Ferrari, build an extension to your condo and finally take that holiday to the Bahamas.
- Invest in new machinery and get rid of the old crap you used to call assets.
- Put a quality control system in place, because you know [client] can be a little anal.
- Hire a colleague for your lonely engineer and get them to work on [product] v2.0.
- Hire a production manager, poach a marketer and assign a sales director, to free up your time for chasing more [client]s.

Obviously everyone should do something fun and silly like that first point, but as long as they back it up by one or more of the others they can only win. They simply re-invest. They are on the first step of a tricky but rewarding road past the original industry leader(s). They already know how do produce efficiently, they're not burdened by the hassle of developing from scratch and they operate in a mature market well developed by the leaders. According to Blue Ocean Strategy [Kim & Mauborgne] that was a bad place to be... well, that's not so true if you're the underdog.

So where does that leave the current industry leaders? Is there no hope? Up in the ivory tower of quality premium goods, looking down onto the bogs of low-cost copy-cats, they can become overly concerned about keeping the tower intact. That is indeed hopeless. The trick is to realize how to modify the tower and do so in time.

Most businesses understand they need to change the tower by evolving it a little to adapt to changing customer & consumer needs.

Maybe stretch the brand a little and try attracting a new target group. There are a bazillion books out there explaining how to do that, if you aren't doing that already.

True long term success comes from exploiting your ivory tower's high-altitude panoramic view – and look for crumbling towers in other categories. New markets where your proposition would in fact be the underdog, but one that can provide a smart solution to conundrums your Heimat market has already dealt with. Mature markets with a flaw they weren't aware of, yet. Most often the flaw is a poor price/quality ratio, which is exactly what [competitor] is doing to your business right now. Become a game changer. These oceans are Blue, but not *empty* and entering these will almost always involve tearing down competing towers.

In the end it's quite simple ...

When others start moving IN

... you need to move ON

... or they will catch up with you.

In hindsight, every success seems like the result of strategic brilliance.

Once launched, breakthrough innovation has only two possible endpoints:
1) mainstream
2) vintage futurology books

Emotions are irrelevant, right up to the moment they hit you.

Maybe change programs by definition have only a start and no end point. In the end, it's a choice to no longer stand still.

Then again, change for change's sake is mere restlessness.

Banks not providing credit to small businesses will lead to a new generation of healthier businesses that doesn't need banks. Darwin lives on.

Innovation becoming mainstream means that at any given point in time, someone, somewhere, is working on the next inflatable umbrella.

[Not so long ago, "working hard" and "long hours" were seen as a lack of success. What IDIOT spun that around?]

Of course the main reason the Z-Generation is so agile in today's tech world is their fingers are still small enough to operate modern phones

Why are there no futurologists and/or trend agencies in the Fortune500? There should be if they were any good.

Breakthrough only counts after having broken through.

"Less is More" tends to be just less.

Stay true to your roots, your principles & in twenty years people will finally understand what you really are: a stubborn, old fashioned git.

Funny how you need friends, an accountant & cash to set up a small business, but only friends & an accountant to take over a $10Bn empire.

A brand's product portfolio is only as weak as its strongest link.

Keep a close eye on your competition and be guaranteed to overlook the company that will put you AND the competition out of business.

"Best in category" solutions/people/companies were first "not in category". Not "mediocre in category".

Great innovations never perish without worthy successors. Sorry, make that: even great innovations are eventually trumped by better ones.

Try writing a paragraph of text on innovation without using the letter 'i'. And then you notice a second reason that's difficult.

The fast track to success for your big idea is enabling everyone to take credit for it. Just swallow your ego and try to smiling while it happens.

Treat every idea with the certainty there will be another, better one.

The Next Big Thing is very difficult to spot early, simply because it's often disguised as The Current Small Thing.

Wouldn't it be great if your last failure was all due to bad luck and your current success is all thanks to your unique style and talent?

When gathering confidence for doing new things... Remember to stop doing some old things.

The benchmark for new ideas is not what came before, but what comes after.

[There's no stopping an idea whose time has gone.]

Superimposing Henry Ford onto Steve Jobs: "if I'd asked The People what they wanted, they'd have asked for nothing more than a bigger iPod".

Try imagining Steve McQueen racing the streets of Bullitt's San Francisco in a Toyota Prius - innovation suddenly loses some of its shine.

If you suspect a competitor is evolving the category at the fringes, they've probably already revolutionized the core without you noticing.

For every great idea you put your money on, there are at least ten better ones. But don't worry, you'll find that out in hindsight.

Given the low number of historically proven perfect solutions, the one you just came up with will probably be trumped too. Hope it's by you.

For ideas to get noticed on a horizon far away, they'll need to be big. Unless there's a trail of smaller ones leading there.

Put together, a historian and a futurologist know exactly nothing about the present. But the debate will be massively opinionated.

The pixelated, low resolution world of Legoland proves that High Definition is not necessarily the only way forward.

Just when you thought you were finished, your competition shows you you're not even close. And they're thinking the same.

Perfection would be a great goal to pursue, if it weren't for normality improving so fast.

Perfection is grossly overrated as an endpoint in development.

When you (person/business) think you're finally getting good at something, you are in fact starting to flatline at the top of your S-curve.

Great inventions often happen simultaneously in different categories, cultures & continents. New TV formats show it's true for bad ones too.

Candid Camera: try explaining to anyone under 30 why it was either funny or remarkable. They'll probably post your attempt on YouTube.

What does an ideal, perfectly optimized business process look like? From the comfort of your bed, charging money for stuff you're not doing.

Soon, the world will rebel against baristas insisting on placing a lid on your cappuccino before you reach the condiment counter.

Your comfort zone should lie behind you.

Miracles and Puzzles describe exactly the same reality, yet the former elicits passive submission and the latter active curiosity.

In a cab in Toronto... Driving down Avenue Road... Amazed about city planners' lack of inspiration in naming this street.

The problem when "doing nothing" turns out to be the best option is that no one wants to take credit for it.

I love my paper books. They smell nicer than eBooks and I'm pretty confident they'll also outlive the *.opf and *.azw file formats.

How do you explain the concept of a joystick to a Y-Gen without sounding A) old-fashioned B) perverted?

The only way to beat a competitor with a longer term view than yours is bankruptcy. As for them, it's just another battle.

SIR, THIS IS A SOCIAL MEDIA START-UP.THE BUSINESS MODEL IS THAT YOU GIVE ME MONEY.

I think people retiring at 40, 55 or 70 have all spent roughly the same number of hours working. Only those retiring at 30 found a shortcut.

Mobile phones, laptops, work/private life blurring... All mainstream now. Maybe City bankers really are the Avant Garde of trend setters.

You won't believe how small your old comfort zone looks when you return to it a few years later.

Motels. Now there's a category in dire need of some positive reframing.

Just like in Scooby Doo, competition monsters always turn out to be just a person in a suit.

First-time-right breakthrough innovation lives in business books, MBA courses, board rooms and at the end of the rainbow.

The difference between what is 'real' and what is 'authentic' is not what they are but what's driving them.

In retrospect, people will claim to already have heard of your successful idea about a year before you had it.

I hear tuition fees at the University Of Life are now even higher than those at The School Of Hard Knocks.

Revolutionary new products and services, just like any other revolutionaries, destroy as much as they create. Without exception, nor mercy.

Innovation to romantics is complex and mysterious beauty, to rationalists complex yet cerebral fun - meanwhile the empiricists just go do it.

If you implement creativity like a religion, you'll need miracles to be successful.

Differentiating innovation is about transcending category barriers and leaving them for the competition to trip over.

When Y-Gens talk about family babies, they always refer to nephews and nieces. I think Y-Gens will be extinct soon.

Life never gives lemons to people with a citrus juicer close by.

I hope the day caffeine is revealed as lethal, is after it's ended my life enjoying it.

It’s sad when great products are phased out without a proper successor - Concorde, Space Shuttle, Customer Service, Gasoline, Journalism.

Thank god your competitor's innovation projects are not leading anywhere either. It's probably a non-competitor who'll ruin you both.

[When things start falling apart, it seems like 'dignity' is either the first or the last to go.]

The Innovator's Hell: a burning, flaming oven full of happy, fully satisfied consumers.

First Diet, then Health, then Wellness, then Vitality... How many trends are left to go before Perpetual Nirvana?

Why were so few heritage brands created after the 70's? Well, ask any of today's brand managers "Hey, want this job for the next 15 years?"

Plotting strategy only on strengths (and no vision) is like telling a marathon runner to go run as far as possible, without telling where to.

Somewhere out there, someone is making a living out of doing the exact opposite of what you are doing.

What ever happened to the company that made all the beige pigment used in desktop computers? I hope they're OK.

With the number of caesarean births rising fast, there is nothing stopping us humans evolving brains the size of watermelons.

The Entrepreneur Trap: with no one telling you what to do, you're never ever finished.

Innovations that create new jobs also destroy old ones, by definition.

(proof you're wrong) / (proof you're right)

=

(PR expenses)

“Welcome back” and "Welcome home" are a world apart.

Brand innovation tends to be driven by a single person's urge to leave a mark - and then any mark will do.

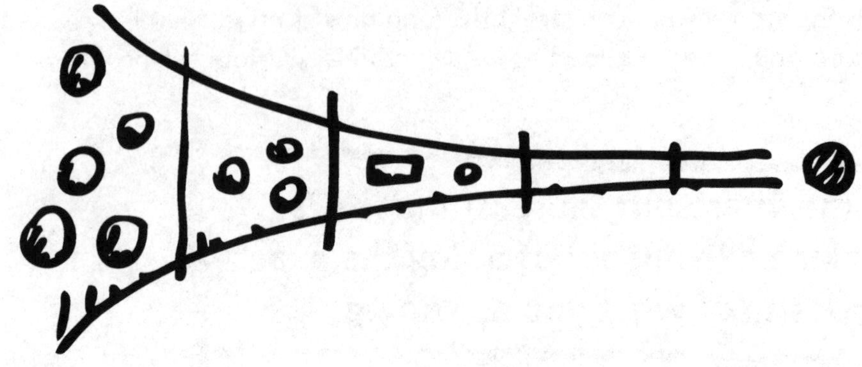

Ceci n'est pas une pipe-ligne d'innovation.

You know you're too old to be a 'high potential' once you realize you're hiring them.

Whatever nearly kills you, doesn't make you stronger. Having nearly killed you, it probably badly damaged and weakened you.

In business, you always have two options: the wrong one, and the uncertain one.

Is it me, or do troubled professionals who visit career coaches have an above average tendency to become career coaches?

From down here on the ground, people with a helicopter view are just noisy specks.

A holistic approach means vertically through the organizational layers, as much as horizontally across disciplines.

I have a hunch that market cycles influence innovation far less than career cycles do.

Yes, I understand you have a vision and dedication. But what you need is an objective and a budget.

Sadly, few things are true 'only because you say so'. Simply not good enough a reason. Except when raising children.

Being underestimated works well on the long term. And vice versa for the exact opposite.

Planning for success is too often forgotten.

Companies succeed even when choosing wrongly, often because competition doesn't choose at all.

Focusing on the competition means that by definition you do not have the initiative.

To anyone complaining how the current string of crises is haltering the upward flow of civilization... our history IS a string of crises.

For some reason, in today's app developing start-ups it is considered a good sign if the company founders are running for the exit. #Bubble

Less is Less, unless you offer More. #Simple

Those little coffee brewers in hotel rooms should be labelled "ONLY IN CASE OF EMERGENCY", just to manage expectations.

Small businesses dream of being big and strong, whilst the big ones wish they were smaller and more agile. Don't we all?

Wrong place at the wrong time? Errr. No, I'd say wrong ingredients at the wrong temperature.

Perfect, Free, Instant and Self-Sustaining - the unbeatable proposition. Just so you know how competition will put you out of business.

I often find "walking away" much more courageous than "sticking with it".

"The world just won't understand the brilliance of my idea" - Stubbornness is a two-way street.

Shopping abroad, we all have small change angst.

Advertising via social media. Imagine your $2m billboard campaign being 'unfriended' with a click of a button.

Let's not be too dramatic about wishing time travel were possible into the distant past. One minute is probably enough for even the stickiest situations.

The Cost-Value Wormhole. When you save so much cost from your A-brand product that it emerges as inferior to the B-brand alternative.

If the time isn't right for your new idea, then find another place, not another time.

Unsolved puzzles of modern Man: squaring the circle - JFK's assassination - superconductivity at room temperature - hotel shower controls.

The smörgåsbord of life usually presents itself like an IKEA canteen.

Eating insects gross? Most people don't like recognizing their meat either. Can't we just grind up grasshoppers and mould them into burgers?

Key to a healthy lifestyle: everything in moderation. Including moderation.

No matter how advanced our technology becomes, humanity will always remain a sucker for coupons.

If you can get away with ordering less than one Venti™ Cappuccino an hour, it's cheaper to live in a Starbucks than in a London City condo.

Of the biggest benefit of staying in a hotel in your home country is that none of the TV channels seem even remotely odd.

Another day, another flight, another 100kgs CO2. Really worried that I'll wake up one morning with a Greenpeace activist chained to my leg.

The fact you don't hear of many successful introverts just shows you don't know who's really running the world around you.

Do NOT eat beef noodles in front of your laptop.

Returning to your old comfort zone is like returning to your home village. Cosy, but everything seems so small & a little old fashioned.

Einstein's theory of relativity and time elasticity can be experienced personally by experimenting with travel with- or without children.

Maybe bio-gas would be more successful if it smelled nicer?

Too many architects forget their designs need to withstand weather and soil - after ten years they look worse than tattoos twice their age.

When pampered people mistake their skewed interpretation of Maslow's Pyramid for being the societal norm, embarrassing things happen.

Assuming perpetually rising productivity, every innovation destroys more jobs than it creates, by definition. #KillerLogic

Don't forget to feed your cash cows or the moving average of private label mediocrity WILL catch up with them.

I have a hunch that success is mostly about managing luck – and then resisting the temptation to gamble.

The closest exit may be behind you #metaphors

It's not about being advanced and innovative. It's about looking incredibly normal and making everything else look hopelessly outdated.

Contrary to Newtonian physics, the centrifugal force in spinning businesses sends the lighter bodies flying out instead of the heavier ones.

If you don't arm your troops with decision making capabilities and simple values, requests become commands, susceptible to noise on the line

[Filters get clogged and become bottlenecks. That is not just an analogy, it is what actually happens with all filters around you.]

What do you call the bit that's left after you sold all the valuable parts of a business?

Is it a platform-quality idea? Well, what do you think are the chances it will outlive you and make your adult grandchildren smile?

Two-way broadcasting is not a conversation.

UGH. SOMEONE WITH HELICOPTER VIEW.

"Customer Success Manager" - that puts the pressure entirely on the wrong person in the equation, no?

Most foresight projects end up becoming insight projects because of how long it takes them to get signed off and started.

"You know what you should do? You should stress less." - the ultimate in useless advice.

Whoever coined the phrase "Talk is cheap" clearly wasn't using a Swiss mobile phone provider.

"Hey, that's an interesting observation! Let's pigeonhole it" - everyone in Western society, since Aristotle.

"Oh you meant a LAUNCH date! I thought you just wanted to get together for a bite to eat." - When executive lunch dates get awkward.

"I'll make him an offer he can't reuse" - Marketing, in a nutshell.

"I didn't buy X for $Y, so I actually earned $Y and can now spend $(Y-10%) on Z and still save money" - Banks, EU-budgets and Girlie Logic.

Complaining implies you're putting control of the solution in someone else's hands. Not a good idea.

Not all market launches cost tons of money. Some also cost you your marriage, health and sanity.

Power is about access, not money.

"Our CEO instructed our team to be more entrepreneurial" - oxymoron

In the grand scheme of things, it's the small schemes that make all the difference.

I AGREE IT'S NOT A VERY LONG TERM OUTLOOK, BUT IT'S WITHIN OUR RESEARCH TEAM'S STATISTICAL CONFIDENCE REQUIREMENTS.

In the canteen of life, we're all handed a wet tray.

"Micro-management" only appears as such when you're on the receiving end.

[What makes you tired by day, keeps you awake at night.]

Inventions we're eagerly waiting for are promised by the experts "within the next 5 years". Yet we never expected the ones we use everyday.

The more complex your strategy, the easier it'll be to post-rationalise all credit towards you, or the blame away from you.

There is only ONE real reason new product launches fail. And the other reason is lack of focus.

In the controlled chaos of doing business, we all get dirty. It's just a question whether it gathers on you or in you.

I tell myself my endless running with luggage & catching flights is today's version of paleolithic me chasing wild boar and hauling it home.

Eager for breakthrough innovation? Ask not how to revolutionise YOUR category, ask how your capabilities can revolutionise ANOTHER category.

"When projects go into the blame-storming phase, too often fingers are pointed at the Boogie" - the Jacksons

Is there a scientific term for panicking over what might happen in case of a panic?

On sports analogies in business: I think they clay tennis court sweeper and the equestrian obstacle hedge trimmer deserve more reference.

"Taking life not too seriously" - FYI this means taking life very seriously. And everything else a lot less.

Now that corporate giants are financially healthier and larger than most countries, I wonder how long before they hand out citizenships?

The main reason there is so little entrepreneurialism in big corporate environments is that no one is confident spelling it.

Are things really getting better or have you merely revised your expectations?

"Let's get our twenty brightest minds together and refine this idea to perfection" – famous last words.

Did you like this little book?

A: "When did you write the book?"
B: "When you were watching TV."

But seriously, assembling & illustrating these thoughts has been an intense pleasure to do. If you enjoyed reading the book, do let me know and I'll include your review in the next print run.

Thank you,

Costas Papaikonomou

Twitter: @grumpyinnovator
Email: costas@grumpyinnovator.com